HOTSPOTS
COSTA

Written and researched by Donna Dailey: updated by Donna Dailey
Front cover photography courtesy of Thomas Cook Tour Operations Ltd

Original design concept by Studio 183 Limited
Series design by BridgewaterBooks
Cover design/artwork by Lee Biggadike, Studio 183 Limited

Produced by the Bridgewater Book Company
The Old Candlemakers, West Street, Lewes, East Sussex BN7 2NZ, United Kingdom
www.bridgewaterbooks.co.uk
Project Editor: Emily Casey Bailey
Project Designer: Lisa McCormick

Published by Thomas Cook Publishing
A division of Thomas Cook Tour Operations Limited
PO Box 227, Units 15-16, Coningsby Road, Peterborough PE3 8SB, United Kingdom
email: books@thomascook.com
www.thomascookpublishing.com
+ 44 (0) 1733 416477

ISBN13:978-1-84157-521-6
ISBN10: 1-84157-521-6

First edition © 2006 Thomas Cook Publishing
Text © 2006 Thomas Cook Publishing
Maps © 2006 Thomas Cook Publishing
Head of Thomas Cook Publishing: Chris Young
Project Editor: Diane Ashmore
Production/DTP Editor: Steven Collins

Printed and bound in Spain by Graficas Cems, Navarra, Spain

All rights reserved. No part of this publication may be reproduced, stored in a retrieval system or transmitted, in any form or by any means, electronic, mechanical, recording or otherwise, in any part of the world, without prior permission of the publisher. Requests for permission should be made to the publisher at the above address.

Although every care has been taken in compiling this publication, and the contents are believed to be correct at the time of printing, Thomas Cook Tour Operations Limited cannot accept any responsibility for errors or omission, however caused, or for changes in details given in the guidebook, or for the consequences of any reliance on the information provided. Descriptions and assessments are based on the author's views and experiences when writing and do not necessarily represent those of Thomas Cook Tour Operations Limited.

CONTENTS

SYMBOLS KEY

The following is a key to the symbols used throughout this book:

i	Information office	**✝**	Church	**🛍**	Shopping
P	Car park	**🚆**	Train station	**🍽**	Restaurant
🚌	Bus stop	**🛡**	Police station	**☕**	Café
☎	Telephone	**✈**	Airport	**🍸**	Bar
✉	Post office	**↘**	Tip	**◉**	Fine dining

t Telephone	**f** Fax	**e** Email	**w** Website address
a Address	**◔** Opening times	**!** Important	

€ Budget price   €€ Mid-range price   €€€ Most expensive

★ Specialist interest   ★★ See if passing   ★★★ Top attraction

INTRODUCTION
Getting to know the Costa Blanca

MEDITERRANEAN
SEA

COSTA
BLANCA

CARTAGENA

MURCIA

ORIHUELA

SANTIAGO DE LA RIBERA

DEHESA DE CAMPOAMOR

TORRE DE LA HORADADA

LA ZENIA

TORREVIEJA

GUARDAMAR
DEL SEGURA

SANTA POLA

ELCHE

ALICANTE

LA MANGA
MAR MENOR

Mar Menor

Atlantic
Ocean

PORTUGAL

SPAIN

COSTA
BLANCA

Mediterranean
Sea

Bay of
Biscay

ANDORRA

FRANCE

MOROCCO

ALGERIA

Getting to know the Costa Blanca

The Costa Blanca – the 'White Coast' – was christened 2500 years ago by Greek traders who founded the colony of Akra Leuka ('White Headland') near today's Alicante. It is a paradise of blue skies, superb beaches, and sun that shines nearly every day of the year. Amid the rocky, sunbaked landscape are fertile river valleys, lush groves of oranges, lemons, olives and almonds, and vineyards producing sweet muscatel grapes.

The Costa Blanca is part of the region of Valencia, which is broken into smaller localities including La Marina Alta (Jávea and Dénia), La Marina Baixa (Benidorm) and Alicante. Each has its own special gastronomy, crafts and fiestas, creating a *calderón* (melting pot) of delightful surprises.

Above all, visitors come to the Costa Blanca for sun and sea. There are 38 Blue Flag beaches – a mark of clean water and top facilities – along this stretch of coast, more than in any other tourist destination in Europe. Some clever soul has worked out that the sun shines on the Costa Blanca for more than 2600 hours every year.

The Costa Blanca has amazing natural beauty lying just behind its beaches. A range of rugged mountains and sculpted peaks creates a spectacular backdrop, less than an hour's drive away. The small villages where life carries on as it has for centuries are a stark contrast to the hedonistic beach scene. In between the terraced mountainsides are valleys fragrant with flowers and wild herbs. Sometimes the mountains wade into the sea, creating tranquil coves beneath precipitous cliffs and landmarks like the striking Peñón de Ifach (see page 20).

MOORISH NAMES

After the Christian re-conquest, many Moors continued to inhabit towns here, until they were officially expelled in 1609. Inland towns still bear traces of this in their ruined castles, architecture and even names: the prefix 'Beni', means 'son of' in Arabic.

On the Costa Blanca there are all sorts of water sports on offer, with several golf courses, and opportunities for adventure sports such as rock-climbing. A wander around one of the old town centres will reveal charming squares, parish churches, narrow streets of immaculate, whitewashed houses or others lined with imposing medieval mansions. There are many ways to explore the Costa Blanca; on coach tours, boat trips, trains and, of course, you can always hire a car.

Fiestas are the heart and soul of the Costa Blanca. Giant statues are set aflame in the town squares, bulls jump into the sea and latter-day Moors and Christians re-enact historic battles, while small local fiestas are marked by costumes, processions and dancing. The Spanish celebrate with dedication and style, and there are festivities around the Costa Blanca at almost any time of year.

COSTA BLANCA IN THE PAST

The Iberians, Greeks and Romans all had settlements on the Costa Blanca, but its strongest influence came from the Arabic Moors, who landed at Gibraltar in AD 711 and held sway over southern Spain for nearly 800 years. They introduced citrus fruits, rice, dates, cotton, and irrigation and terrace farming that enabled the Costa Blanca to thrive.

The other influence on the Costa Blanca was the sea. Coastal villages were often prey to pirate attack, and fortress-churches and windows with heavy iron grilles are still in evidence, along with busy fishing ports.

COSTA BLANCA TODAY

The 1950s and 1960s saw the start of tourist development here. Benidorm, long a British favourite, is mainland Spain's largest resort; from a distance, its high-rise skyline shimmers like a mirage. Benidorm would be a sleepy town of 57,000 were it not for the annual influx of 3.5 million visitors, a third of whom are British. Bitter, Guinness and English breakfast sit side by side with San Miguel and local dishes. Do not expect everyone to speak English, however. There is an increasing number of visitors from the rest of Europe. The locals speak Valencian, one of the country's four main languages, which is similar to Catalan.

The best of the Costa Blanca

BEST BEACHES

Most resorts sport the Blue Flag of excellence. Jávea's wide, sandy Playa Arenal is shallow for a long way out, making it especially good for small children. Dénia has nearly 12 km (7.5 miles) of coastline, with long stretches of sandy beach running north and south of the town. The best beach for people watching is Benidorm's Playa de Levante, backed by an action-packed promenade.

BEST VIEWS

Between the mountains and the sea, there is no shortage of great views on the Costa Blanca. The landmark Peñón de Ifach, at Calpe, is magnificent seen as a silhouette at sunrise, or you can survey the coast from the top of its granite bulk. You can get a perspective on Benidorm's twin beaches from the castle mirador, but the best views of its high-rise skyline can be seen on a boat trip to Isla de Benidorm. Another good viewpoint is near the dolphinarium at Mundomar.

PICTURE POSTCARDS

The eagle's-nest village of Guadalest is extraordinary. The prettiest stroll on the Costa Blanca must be along Alicante's Explanada de España. Benissa goes about its business largely unaffected by tourism, and a walk up Calle Puríssima and the surrounding streets offers a pleasant glimpse of Spanish life past and present. Altea's Plaza de la Iglesia and its steep old-town streets makes another atmospheric spot to while away the hours. Another great place to imagine yourself as part of a postcard is beside one of the magical pools and waterfalls at the Fonts de l'Algar.

BEST ATTRACTIONS

Visit Aqualandia, the biggest water park in Europe and among the best in the world (see page 102). For nightlife, do not miss the glitzy extravaganza of music and dance at Benidorm Palace (see page 32).

RESORTS
Places under the sun

⬤ Cap de la Nao provides good views over Jávea and out to sea

Jávea
the good life

Running between two headlands – Cap Sant Antoni to the north and Cap de la Nao to the south, both with splendid views – Jávea sparkles with signs of the good life. Pockets of orange trees or pine forest conceal smart residential zones hidden in the hills.

THINGS TO SEE & DO
Cap Sant Antoni ★★
From the Old Town, take Calle Virgen de Los Angeles (signposted to Dénia), and turn right at the top of the hill after a series of winding curves (signposted). There is a lighthouse at the end of the road, and viewpoints with great views over Jávea's port, beach and bay.

Cap de la Nao ★★
A pretty coastal drive south of Jávea takes you to the lighthouse at Cap de la Nao. From the lighthouse you will have a good look at the precipitous headland and misty views of the distant mountains. There are a couple of bar-restaurants for refreshments. Back on the main road, you can carry on to Granadella, passing through a forest with shady spots for a picnic. The area is popular for hiking. The road ends at the tiny village, where there is an equally tiny – but very busy – pebble beach of large white stones. It has a beach bar, sunbeds and thatched umbrellas.

The Old Town ★★
At the heart of Jávea's Old Town is the Gothic fortress church of San Bartolomé, surrounded by medieval houses. The archaeological museum has a small but good collection of artefacts spanning several eras, and is housed in a beautiful 17th-century mansion. **Museum** 🄐 Calle San Buenaventura 🕒 Open Mon–Fri 10.00–13.00 and 18.00–21.00, Sat and Sun 10.00–13.00 ❶ Admission free. A good place to pick up tasty cheeses and cold meats is the **indoor market**. 🕒 Open Mon–Fri 08.00–13.30 and 17.00–21.00, Sat 08.00–14.00, closed Sun

Children

Every evening, there is a funfair with games and rides on Paseo Amanecer, opposite the Arenal beach. Next door is a small go-karting track. Or catch the tourist train (evenings) for a ride around town.

BEACHES

The best swimming beach is the wide, sandy Playa Arenal, with shallow water and gentle waves. In the evening, local artisans set up a good crafts market along the promenade. Playa de la Grava is a narrow, pebbly beach stretching out from Jávea's small port. Halfway along, the large rock ledge jutting out into the sea makes a peaceful spot. The pretty tiled promenade is a nice place to join the locals for a late afternoon or evening stroll.

SHOPPING

Cristobel Specialists in fine-quality, engraved glassware. ⓐ Corner of Calle Roques and M Gallard, across from the municipal market ☎ 96 646 0257

Decuero Handmade belts, bags, wallets and leather goods, some handpainted. ⓐ Plaça de la Iglesia in the Old Town ☎ 96 579 3706 ⏱ Closed Sat afternoon and Sun

Jakarta One of the best gift shops on the Costa Blanca. Stylish sun-dresses, T-shirts, skirts and trendy beachwear. Arty gifts such as painted wooden cats, decorative mirrors, great jewellery. ⓐ Paseo Amanecer, Playa Arenal ☎ 96 579 3851

Mercadona Jávea's biggest supermarket ⓐ Avenida de Pla, the main road between the Old Town and Arenal

La Pallissa Lladró, glassware, dolls, mirrors and comical statues and figurines. ⓐ Paseo Amanecer, Playa Arenal ☎ 96 647 0618 ⏱ Closed Sun

Polly's Bookshop A good selection of secondhand English books. ⓐ Across from the port tourist office ⏱ Closed Sun

RESTAURANTS

Casita de Paco €€–€€€ The speciality here is *fideua*, a regional dish of tiny spaghetti cooked in a fish stock. ③ Jávea–Gata road, just before Benitachell crossing ❶ 96 579 5909 ⏱ Closed Tues in winter

El Clavo € Authentic fishermen's bar at the port, serving tapas and fresh fish. ③ Bastarreche 15 ❶ 96 579 1014 ⏱ Closed Wed

Gota del Mar €€€ Tastefully decorated, excellent service, French and Italian cuisine, with splendid views. ③ Urb. Cap Marti 531, next to the Urb el Tosalet, on the Cabo de la Nao road ❶ 96 577 1648

L'Hellin €€ Set alongside the town's pebble beach, enjoy a cool drink on the terrace of this popular café bar followed by light Mediterranean fare. ③ Avenida Mediterráneo ❶ 96 579 1379

Tasca Tonis € Good regional home cooking using fresh local produce makes this busy restaurant an area favourite. ③ Major 2 ❶ 96 646 1851 ⏱ Closed Sunday afternoon

Restaurante Cristobal Colón €–€€ This busy beachside restaurant features fresh fish caught in the local bay. There is a menu of the day and cheap chicken and spaghetti dishes for children. Friendly waiters. ③ Playa Arenal ❶ 96 647 0958 ⏱ Closed Nov and Dec

NIGHTLIFE

La Llum One of Jávea's hottest night spots. ③ Carrer de Gual 1

Moli Blanc The 'white windmill' disco is huge inside, with an open-air bar and a swimming pool. ③ Calle del Cabo de la Nao ❶ 96 579 0507 ⏱ Open Fri and Sat all year, nightly in summer ❶ Admission charge

Montgó de Bongo Caters for the beach crowd by day, smart dress in the evening. ③ Playa de la Grava ⏱ Open July and Aug only

Moraira
Blue Flag beach

Moraira is a small gem of a resort situated between Jávea and Calpe. A handful of streets rises up behind a pretty harbour filled with yachts. Between the port and the sandy l'Ampolla beach are the remains of an old Moorish castle and a tiny chapel. On the other side of the port, below the Torre-vigía (the old stone watchtower), on top of Cap d'Or, is the beach of El Portet, a Blue Flag beach that is good for water sports.

 The tourist information office is located on the Moraira–Calpe road opposite the beach. ❶ 96 574 5168

RESTAURANTS & BARS

 El Andaluz €€ Regional cuisine and barbecue. Live jazz music. ❶ 96 574 5729

SHOPPING

 There is a lively fish market every morning at the port from 10.00 onwards.

Bodega Carmen Good selection of wines and liqueurs, with little gift bottles of muscatel and other spirits. ❸ Calle Dr Calatayud 28 ❶ Open 09.00–14.00 and 17.00–21.00, closed Sun evening

Ceramica Les Sorts Well-stocked treasure trove of brightly hued pottery from around the region. ❸ Edif Kristal Mar 18D–18E ❶ 96 574 5737

Vicente Ferrer Fun and unique gifts – photo frames, dolls, ceramics, crafts, kitchenware. ❸ Calle Dr Calatayud 41 ❶ 96 574 4053 ❶ Closed Sun evening (summer); closed Sat evening and Sun (winter)

Saxo € Open-air bar with swing chairs, loud music and promotion evenings with discounts on certain drinks. ⓐ Moraira–Calpe road ⓛ Open daily, eves only (July–Aug); Fri and Sat eves (Sept–June)

Girasol €€€ It is worth the drive into the hills above Moraira to eat at one of the best restaurants in Spain. The superb Mediterranean cuisine is matched only by the views over the hills and coast from the terrace. ⓐ Carretera Moraira-Calpe km 1.5 ⓣ 96 574 4373 ⓛ Open dinner only (July–Aug); lunch and dinner, but closed Sun evening and Mon (Sept–June)

Moraira looks picture perfect, rising from behind a pretty harbour

● *Peñón de Ifach is a nature park (see page 20)*

Calpe
towering volcano

Calpe is dominated by the Peñón de Ifach, the majestic natural landmark of the Costa Blanca shoreline. This volcanic rock rises more than 300 m (990 ft) above sea level like a mini Rock of Gibraltar, and is joined to the mainland by a narrow strip of land. Calpe is a large, busy resort and at first glance its skyline of modern hotel development obscures its origins as an ancient fishing village. Early Iberian tribes settled here, and the Romans founded a prosperous colony.

The port, at the foot of Ifach, is always bustling with fishing boats and pleasure craft, and there are pleasant bars and cafés from which to enjoy the scene. Watch the trawlers return to port after a day at sea to sell off their catch at the lively fish auction. In the Old Town centre you can see typical fishermen's houses along the streets.

THINGS TO SEE & DO
Museo Fester (Fiestas Museum) ★
On show here is a variety of Calpe's colourful costumes and decorations, including those from the Moors and Christians, the Fallas and other celebrations. ⓐ Calle José Antonio ⏰ Open 10.30–13.30 and 18.00–22.00 (summer); Tues–Sun 17.00–20.00 (winter) ⓘ Admission free

The Old Town ★
Calpe's Old Town reveals glimpses of its history and culture. Torreón de la Peça is a defence tower reinforced by the remains of the Old Town walls. Attached to the attractive parish church is the Iglesia Antigua, the region's only standing example of the Gothic-Mudejar architectural style. Near the church is a small **archaeological museum**. ⏰ Open 10.30–13.30 and 18.00–22.00 (summer); Tues–Sun 17.00–20.00 (winter) ⓘ Admission free. Arrabal is the old Moorish quarter of steep, narrow streets and small whitewashed houses; the pavement stones display anchors, geometrical drawings and other motifs typical of Calpe.

Peñón de Ifach ★★

The towering rock has been turned into a nature park. Peregrine falcons and a large colony of seagulls nest in the rock walls. The **Nature Room** contains exhibits about the park. You can climb to the summit (allow up to an hour) on a pathway tunnelled through the solid rock, for a marvellous view of the coastline. On a clear day you can see the island of Ibiza. ☎ 96 597 2015 ◐ Open Mon–Fri 08.00–19.00, Sat–Sun 08.00–16.00 (summer); Mon–Fri 08.00–18.00, Sat–Sun 09.00–15.00 (winter)

 As you wander around the Old Town, look out for the mosaics and murals decorating the house facades.

BEACHES

Calpe has three good sandy beaches. La Fossa-Levante lies at the base of Ifach, running north and east into the next beach, Playa Calalga. The third, Playa Arenal-Bol, runs west from the port to the Old Town.

RESTAURANTS

Pizzeria Campanari €€ This friendly pizzeria offers a wide variety of Italian-inspired food, from rich pasta dishes to succulent oven-baked lamb. ❸ Calle Campanario 18–20, in a narrow alleyway just off the Plaça de España ☎ 96 583 3231 ◐ Open 18.30–midnight

 Los Zapatos €€€ One of Calpe's oldest established restaurants, serving international haute cuisine. A gourmet heaven of superb food and fine wines. ❸ Calle Santa María 7 ☎ 96 583 1507 ◐ Open evenings 19.00–23.30, lunch 12.30–15.00, closed Tues–Wed ❶ Be sure to reserve a table well in advance. Wheelchair friendly

---

SHOPPING

Calpe's weekly market takes place on a Saturday on the northern outskirts of the Old Town.

Albir
tranquil and inviting

A mere 6 km (3.5 miles) from Benidorm lies the calm oasis of Albir, its long stretch of pebble beach separated from the larger town by a series of rugged cliffs and tiny coves. Though now a modern tourist resort of international character, Albir is linked to the inland town of L'Alfàs del Pi, which has retained its unspoilt rural character.

Fragrant orange and lemon groves, along with pink-blossomed almonds, fill the fields around L'Alfàs del Pi, but the symbol of the town is a different tree: the ubiquitous Mediterranean pine that provides welcome shade in summer and adds so much to the region's scenic quality. Such is the town's winning charm that many visitors from abroad have settled in the area permanently – hence the large number of excellent restaurants and cafés catering to the town's Dutch, Norwegian, German and British residents.

THINGS TO SEE & DO
Casa de la Cultura ★
Check out events at the town's House of Culture, which is the setting for plays, rock, jazz and classical concerts and art exhibitions throughout the year. It is also the site for the annual Film Festival (first week of July) and the Jazz Festival (October).

Walking ★★
If you feel adventurous, take a hike along the footpaths of the Sierra Helada, to enjoy the breathtaking views and the plants and flowers that grow on the mountain slopes.

 The tourist office just back from the seafront in Albir is very helpful and can provide hiking maps. ❷ Oscar Esplá 1
❶ 96 686 7022

Waterfalls ★

In Callosa d'En Sarrià, 15 km (9 miles) from L'Alfàs del Pi, you can take a refreshing shower in a natural waterfall and drink the health-giving waters of the local springs. Another scenic village, noted for its spring-fed fountain of 221 spouts, is Polop, 8 km (5 miles) from L'Alfàs del Pi.

The town's most important festival, in honour of 'Christ of the Wise Choice' is celebrated from 7 to 10 November with parades, processions and floats. The Festival of Creueta (the Little Cross) is held in May and the Summer Feast, celebrating local food and wine, takes place during the first fortnight of August.

RESTAURANTS & BARS

Coco Loco €€ Beachfront cocktail bar with a Caribbean theme, popular with families and all ages. ⓐ Paseo de Estrellas, Playa Albir, L'Alfàs del Pi ⓣ 96 686 6723 ⓛ Open until the small hours in summer

Cuenco de Oro € Excellent-value Chinese and Indonesian restaurant, with an efficient takeaway service. ⓐ Avenida de Oscar Esplá 15, Albi ⓣ 96 686 7450

Enrique €€–€€€ This formal Spanish restaurant, specializing in fresh fish, is perfect for a special occasion. ⓐ Avenida de Oscar Esplá 15 ⓣ 96 686 8098 ⓛ Booking advised in high season

Estrella Polar Pizzeria €–€€ Friendly and relaxing place to enjoy authentic Italian pizza. ⓐ Avenida del Albir 79 ⓣ 96 686 6736 ⓛ Closed Oct–March ⓘ Booking advised in high season

El Galeón €€ Dress up for an evening at this romantic international-style restaurant enjoying the beautiful seafront views. ⓐ Paseo de Estrellas, Playa Albir ⓣ 96 686 5454

Benidorm
Old Town and beaches

Benidorm's beautiful bay is split into two sandy crescents by a rock promontory, once the site of a commanding castle. It is now topped by a tiled mirador or viewpoint, which provides panoramic views from its Mediterranean balcony. The Old Town of narrow streets behind the castle is the Spanish part of Benidorm, though there is no shortage of pubs and cafés run by expat *ingleses*.

BEACHES

Benidorm's twin beaches add up to 5 km (3 miles) of fine golden sand. Most of the action is along the east beach, the Playa de Levante. The pedestrianized promenade (beware of local traffic) stretches east from the Old Town to the foothills of the Sierra Helada at Rincón de Loix and is lined with restaurants and cafés, some with afternoon tea dances and evening entertainment. Look out for the beach sand sculptures, and go there on Sundays to see the locals dressed up for their traditional pre-lunch stroll (*paseo*). Also pleasant for an evening amble, since the noisy discos have all been moved into another area of the town.

The west beach, Playa de Poniente, is longer and less crowded, and its shoreline is rock free. Here you will find a bit more privacy. It is backed by the Parque de Elche, whose breezy palms come from the neighbouring town. Between the two, sheltered by the port and the cliffs of the castle, is the small beach of Mal Pas, where smugglers used to land their cargo. Most of the nautical activities take place here.

You can hire sunbeds and parasols for the day – hang on to your receipt so that you can prove you have paid if asked. There are pedalos for hire at regular intervals along both beaches, which also have children's play areas, volleyball nets and diving platforms.

Take a souvenir snap of Grand Hotel Bali in La Cala, which opened in May 2002. At 210 m (690 ft), it is the tallest hotel in Europe and the tallest building in Spain.

THINGS TO SEE & DO

Aqualandia ★★★

This thrilling water park – said to be the largest in Europe – certainly makes a big splash with visitors. ⓐ Sierra Nevada, Rincón de Loix, Benidorm ⓣ 96 586 4006/7/8 (see page 102)

Bowling Centre ★

Recreation centre with 10-pin bowling, ping-pong, billiards and other games. ⓐ Avenida del Mediterráneo 22, next to Festitron ⓣ 96 585 4187 ⓛ Open 11.00–02.00 ⓘ Fee per game plus shoe hire

Festitron ★

Games arcade for big boys and girls, with large-screen Harley Riders and the like. ⓐ Avenida del Mediterráneo next to Festilandia Park ⓛ Open 10.30–late ⓘ Free entrance, pay per game

SHOPPING

 The shops along Avenida del Mediterráneo, and those around or near Triangular Square in the old quarter have several leather shops and the small shopping bazaars sell cheap T-shirts, beachwear and sun-dresses.

Arte Estudio Lucas A tiny old-town studio-shop. The artist specializes in painting coats of arms, and sells pretty paintings of the sea. ⓐ Calle del Mal Pas, opposite the church ☎ 96 585 8914

Bodega El Barril Good range of booze at competitive prices. ⓐ Avenida del Mediterráneo 37 ☎ 96 585 9018 🕐 Closed Sun

Bordados Rodríguez Beautiful embroidered tablecloths, serviettes and other top quality goods. ⓐ Avenida Martínez Alejos 5, in the Old Town 🕐 Closed Sun

Casa de Cinturón Good-quality leather goods – bags and belts. ⓐ Avenida del Mediterráneo 18 ☎ 96 585 0144 🕐 Closed Sun

Carrefour A hypermarket. Bus no 12 runs from Rincón de Loix hourly (09.30–12.30 and 16.30–19.30). ⓐ Off the Benidorm bypass 🕐 Open Mon–Sat 10.00–22.00 and Sun in high season

La Marina Shopping Centre Costa Blanca's largest shopping mall. Free basement parking plus three floors of fashion, electrical goods, jewellers, lingerie, opticians and cameras. The third floor features terraced restaurants, bars and a nine-screen cinema. ⓐ Behind Carrefour hypermarket on La Marina Commercial Estate 🕐 Open seven days a week.

Maryfra There are several branches selling popular colognes, creams and cosmetics, usually discounted. ⓐ Calle Gambo 3 and 10; also at Calle Gerona 46 ☎ 96 585 4935 🕐 Closed Sun

Mercado Indoor market with stalls selling fresh fruit, vegetables, fish, meat and baked goods, as well as some clothes and souvenirs. ⓐ Avenida L'Ametlla de Mar 🕐 Open Mon–Sat 08.30–15.00 and 17.00–21.00, closed Sun

Mercadona Supermarket. ⓐ Avenida Alfonso Puchades (served by buses no. 1 and no. 8) 🕐 Open Mon–Sat 10.00–20.30

Mediterráneo Park ★

Another children's funfair. ⓐ Avenida de Mallorca, on the opposite side of Avenida del Mediterráneo ⓛ Open 19.30–01.00 ⓘ Pay per ride

Mundomar ★★★

Next door to Aqualandia, the Costa Blanca's 'Seaworld' also has a colourful array of toucans, flamingoes, bats and birds. Dolphins perform twice a day in the dolphinarium, and the parrots and sea lions also put on a show. ⓐ Sierra Nevada, Rincón de Loix, Benidorm ⓣ 96 586 9101/2/3 (see page 102)

Museo de Cera ★★

Meet Elvis, Dracula and a host of other familiar faces at Benidorm's wax museum. Dads may also enjoy the Old Lead Soldiers Museum, with more than 2000 figures from many conflicts and countries. ⓐ Avenida del Mediterráneo 8 ⓣ 96 680 8421 ⓛ Open 11.00–01.00 (summer); 10.00–21.00 (winter) ⓘ Admission charge

⬇ *Dolphins perform at Mundomar*

⬤ *Terra Mítica features an Egyptian Gate*

Sightseeing Trains ★★
Mini-trains depart outside the funfairs for a 25-minute ride around the Levante Beach. ⏱ Open until late ❶ Admission charge

Terra Mítica ★★★
Over a million square metres of theme park based on the ancient civilizations of Egypt, Iberia, Rome, Greece and the Barbary Coast. The huge complex and its great stone constructions, including the Acropolis, the Coliseum and the Land of the Pharaohs, also features top-class theme restaurants and hi-tech rides such as the largest wooden roller coaster in Europe, the Cataracts of the Nile and the rapid swoop to earth of the Flight of the Phoenix. Miniature versions of all rides are available for young children. ❸ Just outside Benidorm (park has its own bus and train service) ❶ 90 202 0220 ⓦ www.terramiticapark.com. ⏱ Open daily 10.00–20.00 (June–mid-Sept); until midnight (mid-July–early Sept); varying days 10.00–20.00 (mid-March–June and mid-Sept–Oct); closed (Nov–mid-March) ❶ €33 adults, €25 children aged 5–10, children aged 4 and under free; discounts for groups and senior citizens; a two-day ticket covers it all; paid parking is available

Water sports

During high season the **Cable Ski** operates at the Rincón de Loix end of Playa Levante (**①** 96 585 1386). Or hire a boat from **Carlos Launch Rental** at the port (**①** 96 585 3018).

TOURS
Calpe boat trip ★★

For the best views of the coastline, take a boat ride from Benidorm to Calpe (see page 18). There is time to wander around the port beneath the majestic Peñón de Ifach before your return journey. Boat trips operate in summer only. Contact the tourist office for further details.

Isla de Benidorm (Peacock Island) ★★

Visit that mysterious rock looming offshore, popularly known as Peacock Island because of the aviary there. The ten-minute boat ride from the port provides you with splendid views of Benidorm's skyline. The waters around the island are a marine reserve, and you can journey beneath the waves in the Aquascope for a mesmerizing look at the schools of fish and colourful underwater life. Afterwards you can visit the bar or the peacock aviary, or hike the island trails. Boats return to Benidorm roughly every hour.

The Lemon Express ★★

A trip from Benidorm to Gata de Gorgos on this jolly green train is the Costa Blanca's most popular tour, named after the lemon groves that once stretched to Altea. The single-track train reveals stunning coastal scenery as it winds its way through tunnels and along narrow ravines high above the sparkling sea, until it reaches Gata (see page 64), where you will have a quick tour of one of Spain's most popular guitar factories. Gata is known for its basketry and wickerwork, and there is time to visit shops selling these local handicrafts. A rollicking ride home is enhanced by free-flowing Lemon Express *cava* (sparkling wine). Ask for details at your hotel or book directly. **➋** The train leaves from Benidorm station **①** 96 680 3103 **🕒** Runs Tues–Sat

EXCURSION
Cuevas de Canalobre

Unlike many caves, which are the geological equivalent of damp dungeons, at 70 m (230 ft) high, this ornate cavern has one of the highest vaults in Spain, with a year-round constant temperature of 18°C (64°F). Estimated to be around seven million years old, this collection of weirdly shaped stalagmites and stalactites was discovered in the 8th century by the Moors; more recently it was used as a secret aircraft engine factory during the Civil War. There is a guided tour set to a background of classical music, which gives it a cathedral-like feel – the acoustics are so good. ⓐ Busot, 24 km (15 miles)

ⓐ The beach at Benidorm

east of Alicante, 40 km (25 miles) west of Benidorm ⓣ 96 569 9250 ⓛ Open daily 10.30–19.50 (Easter and mid-June–Sept); 11.00–17.50 (Oct–early-June); guided tours every 30–40 minutes; concerts often take place here March–April and Nov–Dec ⓘ Admission charge

---

The Cuevas de Canalobre is a popular tourist destination, so it is a good idea to go later in the day if you want to visit in smaller groups. You could stop off on the way back for dinner at the family-run **Mesón 5 Hermanos** (€). It specializes in paella, chargrilled meats and *conejo al ajillo* (garlic rabbit). ⓐ on the road towards Busot. ⓣ 96 569 9102

RESTAURANTS & BARS (see map on page 24)

Aitona €€–€€€ ❶ Look for the giant prawn and paella pan advertising this fish restaurant, which also serves meats and paellas. ❸ Calle Ruzafa, Old Town ❶ 96 585 3010

La Cava Aragonesa €€ ❷ Pleasant bar with possibly the best tapas in town. Dishes are displayed in a glass counter, below the hanging hams. Champagne and wines. ❸ Plaza de la Constitución, Old Town ❶ 96 680 1206

Churchill's €–€€ ❸ Traditional 'olde worlde' pub. Live music every night. ❸ Calle Lepanto

Eduardo's Piano Bar € ❹ Some of the best prices in town. A San Miguel or a coffee and brandy on the patio at happy hour will cost you so little, you will be amazed. At night, Eduardo takes to the keyboards and everybody sings along. It is tucked away down a short passageway, so look for the signboard beside the open-air souvenir shop. ❸ Avenida del Mediterráneo between Avdas Cuenca and Mallorca ◷ Happy hour 10.30–19.30; singalong from 21.30, closed Aug

I Fratelli €€ ❺ Long-standing and popular Italian restaurant that serves seafood and lamb dishes along with a good selection of pastas. Fresh fish baked in a salt crust is a favourite. Attractive dining room is decorated with an art deco flare. ❸ Avenida dr Orts Llorca 20 ❶ 96 585 3979 ◷ Closed Wed (winter)

Ku Beach Bar €€ ❻ Shady terrace café-bar with submarine sandwiches, baguettes or *chapatas*. Also burgers and salads. ❸ Ku Beach Hotel, Avenida de Alcoy, on the promenade ❶ 96 586 8232

Magic Roundabout €–€€ ❼ Popular for its British-style food, especially Sunday lunch. ❸ Calle Ibiza ❶ 96 585 1839

Mesón del Jamón €–€€€ **8** The 'House of Ham' is a typical Spanish restaurant with cured hams hanging from the ceiling and a refrigerated display from which you choose your fish or meat before it is cooked. **a** Calle Gerona 6/7 **t** 96 585 2493

Ray's Fish & Chips € **9** Serves just what it says, along with scampi, chicken, sausage and fish fingers. **a** Calle Derramador **Open** noon–23.00

Sinatra's €€ **10** A fun disco-pub – trendy, spacious and more upmarket than most. **a** Calle Mallorca

El Tapeo Andaluz €€ **11** This authentic Spanish restaurant is a whirl of frenetic activity at lunchtime, with an excellent *menú del día* and plenty of traditional dishes. **a** Calle Ibiza 42 **t** 96 680 6899

TexMex Mar €€ **12** This fun place serves red-hot dishes, Mexican style. **a** Pasaje La Gavina 14, Playa de Levante, in the Old Town, just off the beach **t** 96 680 5508 **Open** from 19.00

Tiffany's €€€ **13** Superb food and wines abound in Benidorm's oldest restaurant, which was established by effusive and charming host Vicente in 1973. A tinkling piano accompanies your meal. **a** Avenida del Mediterráneo 51 **t** 96 585 1680 **Evenings** only 19.30–midnight **Smart** dress code.

Vincent's €–€€ **14** Benidorm's first British-style pub chain, founded in 1965. Serves traditional English pub grub and there is 'golden oldie' music and karaoke in the evenings. **a** Calle Lepanto **Open** 11.00–22.00

NIGHTLIFE

The Levante side has the liveliest entertainment, with a variety of disco pubs and cabaret bars along Avenida del Mediterráneo and Calle Ibiza. Many singers and comedians come from the UK's northern club circuit.

The disco pubs attract a young international set. The main focus is on a pedestrianized walkway, known as the 'square', where Avenida de Mallorca intersects Calle Gerona. Some bars on the Levante beach feature bands playing Spanish music. Entry is usually free but drinks may be more pricey. In the Old Town, Calle Sant Vicent is one of several narrow streets lined with small pubs.

Benidorm Palace €€€ This big, gorgeous, three-hour floorshow is the highlight of Costa Blanca entertainment, featuring glittering Las Vegas-style cabaret acts, Spanish dancers and flamenco, horses, jugglers and magicians. ❸ North-east of town centre ❶ 96 585 1660/61 ◷ Doors open at 21.00, shows run 22.00–01.30. Show days vary ❶ There are tour coaches from Benidorm hotels and several other resorts; admission is good value and includes the first drink; dinner (optional) is also served.

Castle Conde de Alfaz €€€ Feasting and merrymaking, medieval-style, for all ages. Armoured knights on horseback joust and duel before the king and queen. Sing along with court jesters, or descend into the Pit of Terror. ❸ On the outskirts of Benidorm, on the road to Altea ❶ 96 686 5592/3 ◷ Doors open 20.00; show days vary year-round

KM €€€ Ibiza-style disco. Huge, with lavish decor and swimming pool. ❸ Two locations: one on Playa Levante, one on the disco strip, Antigua Carratera, Km 122 ◷ Open 23.00–06.00 (Easter–Oct)

Penelope €€ One of Benidorm's most famous nightclubs offers two locations for dancing the night away. Penelope Beach Club is right on the waterfront on Avenida de Alcoy, with a cocktail bar and late-night disco. Or head for the mega-club Penelope with top DJs and dancers on the disco strip, Antigua Carratera km 122. ◷ Open 23.00–06.00 (summer)

Rich Bitch €€ Drag and comedy featuring Jordan Rivers and company, the club made famous by the BBC TV series *Escape to the Sun*. Show starts at 22.30, but you must book in advance and take your seat by 21.30 or you will lose it to the queues outside. Expect to pay a small cover charge. Rich Bitch memorabilia is on sale and is also offered as raffle prizes. Cameras allowed but no camcorders. ⓐ Calle de Pau 4, Benidorm Old Town ⓣ 66 605 5906

Top of the Pops €€ Well-known disco pub, recently renovated, playing up-to-the-minute sounds. ⓐ Avenida Almería ⓛ Open 21.00 to the early hours ⓘ 'Anything goes' dress code

---

It is wise to ignore the touts who approach you at bars or on the street or beach selling cheap 'gold' chains – they are nothing but fool's gold.

⬤ *Follow a buzzing night of clubbing with a relaxing day on the beach*

Cala de Finestrat
old-world charm

La Cala de Finestrat is a large, sandy cove on the southern outskirts of Benidorm, part of the municipality of Finestrat, which includes the ancient village in the foothills of the Puig Campana mountain 8 km (5 miles) inland. The beach area with its promenades is on a smaller scale to the larger and noisier Benidorm beaches and is highly favoured by the Spanish locals. A large car park provides free all-day parking.

The village of Finestrat (population 950) dates from the Iberian era and was the local centre of olive farming during the Moorish occupation. Olive and almond trees still abound, flowering in early spring to cover the hills in a show of pink and white blossoms. Its narrow streets and multi-coloured houses, climbing to the lookout point of La Hermita, make it one of the most visited villages on the Costa Blanca. Of interest are the 18th-century blue-domed church with its ceiling and wall frescos and the nearby fountains of Font de Molí. For the best local produce, try the **fruit and vegetable markets** held in Finestrat village and La Cala de Finestrat on Fridays. ⏱ Both open around 09.00–14.00

BEACHES

La Cala de Finestrat is one of the best beaches on the Costa Blanca, a fine sweep of sheltered sand, with a promenade lined by shops, cafés and restaurants. Sunbeds and sunshades are for hire, as well as pedalos.

If you are in Finestrat during August, join the St Bartholomew festivities. From 22 to 25 August, the village throngs with crowds enjoying good local food and wine, as well as processions and fireworks.

RESTAURANTS

El Arenal €–€€ Perennially popular for its seafood paella, this Spanish restaurant on the seafront has a shaded terrace on which to enjoy a leisurely meal. ❸ Avenida Marina Baixa, La Cala Finestrat ❶ 96 585 6700 ❺ Closed mid-Dec–mid-Jan

La Morena €€ An exquisite family-run restaurant set amid almond and olive groves, with excellent cuisine. Specializes in fresh fish, *cabrito* (kid) and tender young lamb. Large range of local and national wines. ❸ Carretera Benidorm, 8 km (5 miles) inland, outside Finestrat village ❶ 96 587 8539 ❺ Open Tues–Sat 13.00–16.00 and 20.00–23.30, closed Mon ❶ Reservations recommended

El Pescador €€ This restaurant has stunning sea views and is popular for lunch. Specializes in fresh local fish and is famous for its hundreds of varieties of traditional local rice dishes. Very good steaks. ❸ At the far end of La Cala beach ❺ Open lunchtime and evenings

NIGHTLIFE

Bounders A lively English-style pub, with karaoke every night (from 21.00 until late) and major sporting events shown on satellite TV. As well as the excellent bar snacks, try the popular Sunday lunch. ❸ Avenida Marina Baixa, La Cala Finestrat

❹ *Finestrat village is south of Benidorm*

Villajoyosa
colourful fishing village

Villajoyosa's capital of the Marina Baixa district, has two distinct areas – a quaint old village and a modern industrial centre. Like many of the towns along the coast, Villajoyosa depends partly on fishing for its income – each day's catch is auctioned off in the late afternoon at the port.

The narrow streets of the old quarter have real character, with rainbow-coloured houses fanning out from the Church of Our Lady of the Assumption and along the seafront. The facades are deliberately painted in bright colours so that they are visible to sailors out at sea. It is a lovely area to wander around – stop for lunch at one of the many restaurants around Plaza San Pedro.

 The tourist office in Villajoyosa is at the top of the Old Town, just off the main road. ❸ Avenida País Valenciá 10 ❶ 96 685 1371

THINGS TO SEE & DO
Fiestas ★★
Villajoyosa's Moors and Christians fiesta in the last week of July turns the streets into a parade ground of marching bands and colourful costumes.

BEACHES
Villajoyosa has 3.5 km (2 miles) of relatively uncrowded beaches. The longest and most central is the Blue Flag Playa Centro, which has fine, pale sand and runs from the old quarter up to the port. Nudists favour the isolated Playa del Racó Conill, 3 km (2 miles) out of town towards Benidorm.

Villajoyosa is famous for its chocolate-making industry – be sure to try some while you are here.

🔺 *Villajoyosa beach*

RESTAURANTS

 Restaurante Madrid €€ This restaurant specializes in seafood, and is a good choice for trying *arroz abanda* or *caldero*. ⓐ Calle Arsenal 1 ❶ 96 589 4249

 Rincón de Cádiz €€ The little terrace overlooking the square is a great place to work your way through a sample platter of the local catch: *merluza* (hake), *boquerones* (anchovies), *emperador* (emperor fish), *sardinas* (sardines) as well as seafood paella. There is also a tasty (and abundant) *menú del día* and excellent *gazpacho*. ⓐ Paseo del Doctor Esquerdo 12 ❶ 96 589 5104 ❶ Closed Tues (winter)

SHOPPING

Villajoyosa's weekly market takes place on Thursday mornings on the northern side of town.

Santa Pola
lively fishing port

Famous as a fishing port since Roman times, Santa Pola is now popular with holidaymakers for its beautiful sandy beaches. They do not suffer from the chock-a-block feel of some of the bigger resorts and are protected from easterly winds by the lighthouse-topped cape, 3 km (2 miles) north-east of town.

THINGS TO SEE & DO
Aquarium ★★

This small aquarium offers a good window on the Mediterranean with close-ups of the ferocious-looking sea snakes, the graceful sea turtle and the Med's only tropical fish, the glamorous blue, gold and orange *pez verde*. ❷ Plaza Fco, Fernández Ordóñez ❶ 96 541 6916 ◐ Open Tues–Sat 11.00–13.00 and 18.00–22.00 (summer); 10.00–13.00 and 17.00–19.00 (winter); Sun 10.00–13.00 ❶ Admission charge

Castle and Maritime Museum ★

The impressive 16th-century castle houses a museum that pays homage to the role of the sea in the life of Santa Pola. ❸ Plaza del Castillo ❶ 96 669 1532 ◐ Open Tues–Sat 11.00–13.00 and 18.00–22.00 (summer); Tues–Sat 11.00–13.00 and 16.00–19.00 (winter); Sun 11.00–13.30 ❶ Admission charge

Isla de Tabarca ★★

This car-free island is a pleasant half-hour boat ride from Santa Pola. Once a pirates' stronghold, Tabarca is now a marine reserve, which makes it a top spot for snorkelling. The island is only 2 km (1.25 miles) long and around 400 m (435 yd) wide, so you can walk right around it, wander through the walled village or sample the local speciality of *caldero*, a rice dish made with fish stock, cooked in an iron pot. In high season boats run roughly every half an hour (09.30–19.30 hours) from Santa Pola's port, much less frequently in winter (❶ 96 541 1113 for times).

 The castle at Santa Pola

SHOPPING

Santa Pola's local market takes place on Monday and Saturday mornings off Plaza de la Diputación.

Pola Park ★

Children will love Pola Park, a large amusement park complete with
bumper cars, roller coasters and all manner of stomach-churning
fairground rides. ⓐ Avenida Zaragoza ⏰ Open 19.30–02.00 (summer);
weekends only 17.00–23.00 (winter) ⓘ Free entry, pay per ride (see also
Rio Safari, near Elche, page 82)

Salt flats ★

Take a drive south towards Cartagena past the *salinas*, salt flats
that yield up the huge white mountains adorning the grounds of
the nearby salt refineries. The lakes are home to a large population
of flamingos.

BEACHES

The long, sandy beaches to the west (Playa Libre, Tamarit – Blue Flag –
Playa Lissa and Gran Playa) are particularly suitable for children because
the water is shallow for a long way out. East of Santa Pola are two more
Blue Flag beaches – the central Playa Levante, and Playa Varadero on the
eastern edge of the town.

RESTAURANTS

Gelatería Miami €€–€€€ Delicious ice creams, waffles and
freshly made crêpes with every topping under the sun are served
up at shady outdoor tables. ⓐ Calle del Muelle

Restaurante Polamar €€ This lively beachside bar serves a good
selection of tapas and sandwiches on a huge sunny terrace. The
cool, upmarket restaurant inside the adjoining hotel specializes in fish
dishes. ⓐ Playa de Levante ⓣ 96 541 3200

16 July is the fiesta of Virgen del Carmen, and from 1 to 8
September, a week-long festival in honour of La Virgen de Loreto
sees a kaleidoscope of fireworks, processions and floats.

Guardamar del Segura
pine forests and dunes

Topped by the ruins of a 13th-century castle, the small town of Guardamar del Segura, which was formerly a fishing village, is surrounded by scenic beaches and sand dunes. The sand dunes themselves were planted with pines, palms and eucalyptus trees at the beginning of the 20th century to stop the moving sand from swallowing up the town.

BEACHES

Guardamar del Segura has five long, sandy beaches. The two nearest to the town centre, La Roqueta and Playa Centro, have all the usual facilities – umbrellas, sun-loungers and pedalos.

However, if you fancy escaping from all of the high-season holiday-makers for an hour or two, head north to Playa Vivers. The pretty beach here is uncommercialized and uncrowded, lined by a row of quaint fishermen's cottages. The beach is backed by the Dunas de Guardamar, a beautiful, shady forest of pines and palms that is perfect for picnics.

RESTAURANT

Beach Bar Casablanca €€ Situated just beyond Playa Roqueta, overlooking the beach, this efficient restaurant serves something for everyone, from full-blown meat and fish dishes to omelettes, pasta and paella and a large choice of salads and burgers. ⓐ Avenida Perú 2 ⓘ 96 672 5822

February is the month of the lively and colourful *carnaval* in Guardamar del Segura – Easter Week sees a host of ceremonial and religious processions, the Moors and Christians make their appearance in the last two weeks of July, and 7 October is a fiesta for the town's patron saint, the Virgen del Rosario.

La Manga & Mar Menor
fun aquatic playground

Mar Menor (literally 'the minor sea') is separated from the Mediterranean by a thin strip of land about 21 km (13 miles) long, known as La Manga. This has the effect of turning Mar Menor into a huge swimming pool with warm, calm waters – the water temperature rarely drops below 18°C (64°F), even in winter. This is where people come to play: there are all kinds of water sports on offer, from sailing to diving and windsurfing, as well as huge stretches of fine white sand for dedicated sun-worshippers.

As you are driving around this area, make sure you look out for windmills – some are in a sorry state, but others have been restored to their former glory.

THINGS TO SEE & DO
Bike riding and walking

The tourist office right at the beginning of La Manga (☎ 96 814 6136) has a brochure of cycling and walking itineraries (look for a blue and white building near a sloping tower topped by a sphere).

Diving ⋆

The area around the lighthouse, Cabo de Palos, is renowned for its excellent diving. There are several diving schools nearby, including the **Club Islas Hormigas**. ⓐ Los Belones ☎ 96 817 5000, ext 1360

Golf ⋆

Golf at La Manga Club: Internationally famous for its three championship golf courses, this exclusive sport and leisure resort also offers horse riding, tennis, squash and bowls. ☎ 96 833 1234

● *Golf at La Manga*

Sailing and windsurfing ★

Manga Surf: This friendly school with English-speaking instructors offers private windsurfing and sailing lessons at affordable prices. If you already know what you are doing, you can just hire the boards or catamarans, or opt for a less technical paddle about in a canoe or pedalo.

ⓐ Gran Vía, exit 23 ⓣ 96 814 5331 ⓛ Open 09.00–21.00

BEACHES

If you are in search of solitude, Calblanque, a few kilometres before la Manga, is the place to head for. A very rough 5 km (3 mile) track keeps all but the most determined peace-seekers away, but the long stretch of near-empty terracotta sand backed by rocky cliffs (no facilities) is worth the tortuous drive. There are white sandy beaches all along La Manga. On the mainland side, the Blue Flag beach of Santiago de la Ribera has good facilities.

 The high concentration of salt and iodine in Mar Menor is said to be highly beneficial to anyone suffering from skin complaints.

⬧ *Windsurfing on Mar Menor*

EXCURSIONS
Out & about

Valencia
rich in history

Valencia, founded by the Romans, became one of the biggest and richest cities in medieval Spain thanks to its fine harbour. Today it is the country's third-largest city and a regional capital, with many monuments and museums.

◆ *Valencia Cathedral, Plaza de la Reina*

Valencia can be visited on a tour from resorts on the Costa Blanca, or independently by bus or car. Along the way you will see terraced fields of olive and almond trees, rice fields and the orange and lemon groves for which the province is known. Tours normally stop en route at the Lladró factory outlet store and take you to the cathedral, the Fallas Museum and El Corte Inglés, Spain's largest chain of department stores.

THINGS TO SEE & DO

Valencia is huge, and you will not be able to cover all of its monuments and sights on one tour. Those listed in this first section are the ones normally visited on an organized tour. The second section (Exploring on Your Own, see page 51) contains suggestions for worthwhile visits to other attractions if you are making your own way. You will need a good map if you want to explore on your own, which you can obtain from one of the tourist offices.

Valencia tourist offices are open Mon–Sat 10.00–18.30:
ⓐ Calle Paz 48 ☏ 96 398 6422; ⓐ At the train station, Estación del
Norte, Játiva 24 ☏ 96 352 8573; ⓐ Plaza Ayuntamiento 1 ☏ 96 351 0417;
ⓐ Calle Poeta Querol ☏ 96 351 4907

The cathedral ★★★

Built on the site of an Arab mosque, Valencia's cathedral took 350 years
to construct and reflects Romanesque, Gothic, baroque and Renaissance
styles. It claims to possess the Holy Grail, said to have been brought here
from Jerusalem in the 13th century. The alabaster stone cup is encased
in glass in the Capilla del Santo Caliz. Alongside is the cathedral
museum. You can also climb the 207 steps to the top of the bell tower,
the Miguelete Tower, for a view over the city. ⓐ Plaza de la Reina
🕒 Cathedral open 07.15–13.00 and 16.30–20.00;. Miguelete Tower open
10.30–12.30 and 16.30–19.00 (until 18.00 in winter) 🛈 Cathedral
museum, admission charge

Near the cathedral

Behind the cathedral in the Plaza de la Virgen is the smaller Basilica of
La Virgen de los Desamparados (Our Lady of the Forsaken), dedicated
to the protector of Valencia. 🕒 Open 07.00–14.00 and 16.00–21.00

Return to the Plaza de la Reina (the coach drop-off point) and turn
right at the *croissanteria* for a closer look at the soaring tower of Santa
Catalina church. A bit further on is Plaza Lope de Vega, where, off a side
alley, you will find the little Plaza Redonda, a circle of old, tiled market
stalls selling fabrics and ceramics around a fountain. 🕒 Closed Sun

Carry on to the busy Plaza del Mercado and turn right to reach La
Lonja de la Seda, the Old Silk Exchange. This huge 15th-century Gothic
building is classified as a UNESCO World Heritage Site, and is now used
for exhibitions. 🕒 Closed Mon, and Sun afternoon 🛈 Admission free

Opposite is the Mercat Central (Central Market), with its modernist-
style facade, tiled dome and stained glass windows. This is the place to

◗ *Shopping in the stylish Mercat Central*

come to buy olives as big as plums, huge chunks of watermelon and giant, sun-kissed peaches. ⏰ Open Mon–Sat

Museo Fallero (Fallas Museum) ★★★

Artists work year round to create giant satirical papier-mâché figures, which are paraded through the streets and burned on the last night of Valencia's main festival, the *fallas*. This humorous museum houses a collection of some of these, dating from 1934 to the present day. Offerings include Indiana Jones, Yoda and Jacques Cousteau as well as Samurai tourists and wrinkled, picnicking pensioners. ⓐ Plaza Monteolivete
☎ 96 352 5478 ⏰ Open Tues–Sat 09.15–14.00 and 16.30–20.00, Sun 09.15–14.00 ⓘ Admission charge

SHOPPING

🛍 **El Corte Inglés** This branch of Spain's biggest department store chain is near the tourist office, about a ten-minute walk from Plaza de la Reina. The main entrance (and coach stop) is along Calle Pintor Sorolla. There are restaurants on the top floor and toilets on the second floor.

Lladró Spain's only handmade porcelain factory is world famous. Excursions visit the factory showroom in a town north-west of Valencia (you cannot tour the workshop itself), which features hundreds of porcelain figures in all shapes and sizes. 'Seconds' are sold at discount prices. ⓐ Tabernes Blanque ☎ 96 185 1570 ⏰ Open Mon–Fri 09.30–19.30, Sat 09.30–13.30

Mercat Central See page 49.

Panadería Santa Catalina The 'Casa Del Pan Quemado' (House of the Burnt Bread) opposite the tower may have an unfortunate name but it sells a great selection of freshly baked sweet and savoury snacks. ⓐ Plaza Santa Catalina 7

El Rastro Valencia's largest market – everything from local handicrafts to clothes and food. ⓐ Mestalla, east of the river ⏰ Sundays

Museo Fallero is a 30- to 40-minute walk from the town centre, so it is worth taking a taxi, which will not cost more than the price of a drink and a sandwich. From the museum, the City of Art and Science (see below) is about a ten-minute walk away.

EXPLORING ON YOUR OWN

There is a daily coach service to Valencia from Benidorm that departs from the Ubesa office at Avenida Europa 8. It is best to buy your ticket and reserve your seat at the office the day before. Buses run roughly every two to three hours, at 08.00–21.40 hours. The journey takes just under two hours and leaves you at Valencia's bus station, where you should go upstairs to the ticket office and reserve your seat for the return journey. Bus no 8 from the front of the bus station will take you to Plaza de la Reina in the centre of town. Buy your ticket on the bus.

Ciudad de las Artes y las Ciencias (City of Art and Science) ★★

Valencia's massive cultural, educational and leisure centre lies on the outskirts of the city centre. L'Hemisfèric, a hi-tech, shell-shaped building surrounded by water is already open, alternating planetarium and laser shows with action-packed documentary-style films on giant screens in the IMAX cinema (soundtracks available in English). This huge, hands-on interactive science museum has now been joined by an oceanography park, complete with dolphinarium, and a performing arts and cultural centre. ❸ Arzobispo Mayoral 14 ❶ 90 2100 031 ❶ Open 11.00–22.00

Palacio de Marqués de Dos Aguas (National Ceramics Museum) ★★

The elaborate baroque facade of this 18th-century building opens up on to an ornate mix of grandiose stately home decor and exquisite ceramics. A series of displays traces the history of this traditional Valencian craft from the 13th century onwards, including the famous Manises pottery. Do not miss the Salita de Porcelana with its porcelain-adorned chairs, the Dormitorio del Marqués with the elaborate four-poster bed and marble bath, and the Red Room, where glorious red upholstery contrasts with sea-green walls. There is also a room

● *City of Art and Science*

containing 18th-century carriages. ⓐ Calle Poeta Querol 2 ❶ 96 351 6392
🕑 Open Tues–Sat 10.00–14.00 and 16.00–20.00, Sun 10.00–14.00
❶ Admission charge

RESTAURANTS & BARS (see map on page 46)

Pedestrianized Calle Don Juan de Austria has scores of outdoor cafés and
bars, and ice cream or croissant shops. Try **Casa Bar Mundo** (€) for good
sandwiches. ❶ 96 351 0093. Plaza de la Virgen has several café terraces
where you can cool down with drinks or ice creams. Or try **Cafetería
Roma** (€€) for something more substantial – the service will not bowl
you over, but their generous-sized sandwiches and tapas are good and
fresh. ❶ 96 392 2474

Cafetería Escocia €€ ❶ For those looking for something more
substantial than a snack, this welcoming little restaurant just
around the corner from Plaza de la Virgen offers a reasonably priced
three-course *menú del día*, with the option of eating outside. ⓐ Calle
Caballeros 5 ❶ 96 391 4999 🕑 Closed Sun

Picoteo € ❷ Have a drink with the market traders at the pretty
tiled bar, or watch the locals bustling in and out of the market over
tapas or sandwiches at one of the shaded tables. ⓐ Plaza del Mercado

Restaurante Generalife €€ ❸ This keeps to the same
menú del día format as Cafeteria Escocia but offers some slightly
unusual dishes such as chops with honey and steak with roquefort
sauce as well as regional rice specialities such as *arroz a banda*.
ⓐ Next door to Cafeteria Escocia ❶ 96 391 7899

Taverna El Clot €€ ❹ Tucked away down a narrow street on the
edge of the charming Plaza Redonda, it is well worth paying the
20 per cent supplement for a table outside. It is very busy at lunchtime,
but the four-course set menu and tapas are worth the long wait.
ⓐ Plaza Redonda 1 ❶ 96 391 8123 🕑 Closed Sun

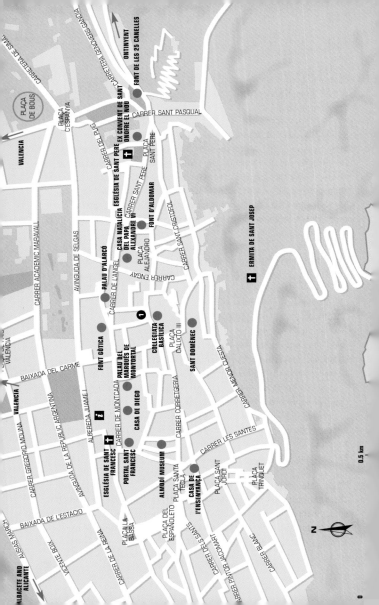

Xátiva
ancient inland town

Xátiva (pronounced 'Sha-tiva'), situated 40 km (25 miles) inland, is reached by a road that winds through a fertile valley of lemon and olive groves up towards the mountains. The Iberians, the Romans and the Carthaginians under Hannibal have all played a part in the history of this ancient town, the site of Europe's first paper mill, built by the Moors in 1150. Today, Xátiva is well known for the many fountains that grace its squares, its attractive old quarter and a magnificent castle perched on the hill overlooking the red roofs of the town below.

 Xátiva is not very well signposted from the coast – follow signs for Albaida to begin with.

THINGS TO SEE & DO
Almodí Museum ★
Housed in a beautiful Renaissance building, this spacious museum contains a variety of archaeological exhibits as well as a collection of predominantly 17th-century paintings by Spanish artists. There are several by José Ribera (El Españoleto) who was born in Xátiva in 1591. Look out for the portrait of the Spanish king Felipe V, which hangs upside down as a symbolic revenge on the monarch for ordering the burning of Xátiva in 1707. Do not miss the lovely cloistered patio. ❸ Calle Corretgeria 46 ❶ 96 227 6597 ❺ Open Tues–Fri 09.30–14.30 (summer); Tues–Fri 10.00–14.00 and 16.00–18.00 (winter); Sat–Sun 10.00–14.00 (year round) ❶ Admission charge

The castle ★★
The imposing, well-preserved walls of Xátiva's castle stretch along the crest of the hill overlooking the town. Although the ridge was fortified as far back as Iberian and Roman times, many of the surviving features date from the Moorish and Gothic eras. A series of impressive gates leads

through the upper castle to a dark prison, a Gothic chapel in which several inmates are buried, and a series of watchtowers with great panoramas over Xátiva and the surrounding valleys. The older, lower castle will also have you whipping out your camera – there is a lovely view back over the main castle from the open balcony in the Queen's Tower, which was named after Himilce, Hannibal's wife, who gave birth to a son here in 218 BC. ● Open Tues–Fri 10.00–19.00 (summer); 10.00–18.00 (winter) ❶ Admission charge

Children
If you are visiting with children, or just plain footsore, a little train leaves from the front of the tourist office to do the rounds of Xátiva's sights. ● Open Tues–Sat 12.30 and 17.30, Sun noon, 13.00, 17.00 and 18.00

Iglesia de Sant Feliu ★
The 13th-century Iglesia de Sant Feliu just below the castle is the oldest church in Xátiva, famed for its Roman columns, Spanish Renaissance paintings and outstanding architecture. ● Open Mon–Sat 10.00–13.00 and 16.00–19.00, Sun 10.00–13.00

Walking tour of the Old Town ★★
A good starting point for a walking tour of the Old Town is Portal Sant Francesc, a square with a baroque fountain. From there, head along the narrow Calle Montcada to the Gothic fountain in front of the 18th-century Palacio de Justicia. Here you can carry straight on past the 13th-century church (Iglesia de San Pedro) to the lovely fountain at the end of the town, where locals queue up to fill all manner of receptacles with the spring water gushing from its 25 spouts.

SHOPPING

Enjoy searching for bargains in the hustle and bustle of the charming marketplace on Tuesday and Friday mornings.

Alternatively, you can take Calle Sanchis to the impressive basilica (La Seu) which was started in 1596, although the main facade was finished in 1920 (🕒 Open for visits Mon–Sat 10.30–13.00). Take a look at the beautiful carving and pillars on the 15th-century hospital opposite. A little further on, steps lead to the market place, an attractive arched square fringed by crumbling facades and wrought-iron balconies. You can end your tour at the Almodí Museum just beyond.

It is no surprise that Xátiva has plenty of churches: two Borgia popes – Calixtus III and Alexander VI – were born in the town in the 14th and 15th centuries.

RESTAURANTS & BARS (see map on page 54)

There are several bars along the Albereda Jaume I that serve sandwiches and snacks at outdoor tables.

La Forca €€ ❶ Locals meander in and out of this attractive tiled restaurant, which specializes in regional cooking, to take away with them huge dishes of paella. The *arroz caldoso*, rice with vegetables, rabbit and chicken, are definitely worth trying, as is the excellent, homemade *flan* (crème caramel). You can also pop in for tapas at the bar. ⓐ Calle Abad Pla ☎ 96 227 3402 🕒 Open Tues–Sun for lunch, Fri and Sat for dinner

BEACHES

If you need to cool off after all that sightseeing, head to the clean, sandy beaches at the coastal town of Gandía (40 km/25 miles from Xátiva).

The Nits al Castell (Nights at the Castle) programme puts on a series of evening performances of ballet, classical music, flamenco and jazz throughout July. Reservations can be made through the tourist office. ⓐ Albereda Jaume 150 ☎ 96 227 3346 🕒 Open Tues–Fri 10.00–14.30 and 17.00–19.00, Sat and Sun 10.00–14.00

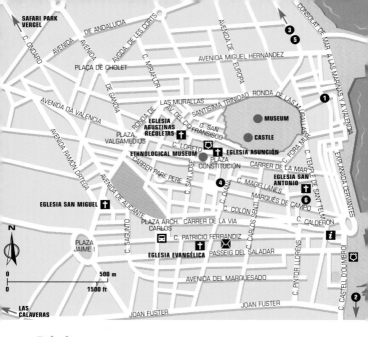

Dénia
something for everyone

With beautiful beaches, a busy port, natural landscapes and an interesting old town to explore, Dénia will keep you occupied for a good while. The castle looming overhead was built during the Islamic era (11th to 12th centuries) – it is a great place to escape from the afternoon heat.

The tourist office near the seafront (ⓐ Plaza Oculista Buigues 9 ☎ 96 642 2367) is very helpful. Ask for their map of the cultural route that takes you along the most picturesque streets. The old Baix de la Mar quarter opposite the port is particularly colourful.

Below the castle, the Town Hall and the Eglesia Asuncíon flank tiny Plaza de la Constitución. From here you can follow Calle Cop, a good shopping street, down to Plaza la Glorieta, a focal point for town festivities. The Marqués de Campo, with its tall canopy of leafy plane trees, leads down to the waterfront. In the evening, stalls selling bags, crafts and jewellery set up along Explanada Cervantes.

 Do not follow the confusing signs to the tourist office – head for the Estación Marítima, or failing that, the port.

THINGS TO SEE & DO
Las Calaveras Cave ★

Tall domes, stalactites and stalagmites mark the 300 m (984 ft) long passage through this prehistoric cave. ❷ 8 km (5 miles) from Gata de Gorgos on the road between Pedreguer and Benidoleig ❸ 96 640 4235 ❶ Admission charge

The castle ★★

It is a steep walk up to the castle, but you can take a train from the station opposite the tourist office. The castle has ruins from the Islamic and medieval periods. It was abandoned in 1859. Today, the enormous grounds seem like a large, shady park, with watchtowers and ramparts to explore and fantastic views over the town and waterfront.

The Governor's Palace at the summit holds a small archaeological museum with Roman coins, artefacts and pottery fragments bearing Arabic motifs. Nearby is a refreshment stand for drinks and ice cream.
Palace and museum ❸ 96 642 0656 ❹ Open 10.00–13.30 and 17.00–20.30 (summer); 10.00–13.30 and 15.00–18.00 (winter) ❶ Admission charge includes entry to the archaeological museum and the ethnological museum in town

Ethnological Museum ★

Dénia's past prosperity from the raisin industry is chronicled in this museum, with photographs and displays portraying the work and lifestyle of that era. ❷ Calle Cavallers 1 ❹ Open Tues–Sat 10.30–13.00, closed Sun evening and Mon ❶ Admission charge (combined ticket including entry to the castle)

Safari Park Vergel ★

Lions, tigers, jaguars, wolves and many other animals roam this small safari park. You can also see huge reptiles, parrots, exotic birds and dolphin-and-seal shows. Horse and camel rides, congo train and other attractions. ❸ On the Vergel–Pego road ☎ 96 643 9808 ⌚ Open 10.00–19.00 (summer); 10.00–17.00 (winter) ❶ Admission charge

Walking

Rising behind Dénia is Mount Montgó (762 m/2500 ft). You can explore it via two hiking routes (guides available from the tourist office). The Ruta Ermitas de Conquista takes you to three hermitages on the lower slopes on an easy two- to three-hour walk. The more difficult climb through El Montgó Natural Park to the top can take all day.

SHOPPING

 Dénia's weekly market displays its wares on Monday mornings, with a small antiques market on Fridays, just around the corner from Plaza Jaime 1. Try also:

Bolsos Paco A good leather shop with reasonable prices. ❸ Calle Patricio Ferrandiz 27 ☎ 96 6421312

Déniabebe Boutique Attractive baby outfits and maternity clothes. ❸ Calle Cop 15 ☎ 96 578 2902 ⌚ Closed Sun

Marsal Shoes and exclusive leather goods plus fabulous swimming costumes, good-value cosmetics and perfumes and upmarket knick-knacks. ❸ Marqués de Campo 28 ⌚ Closed Sun

Mercadillo de Verano The 'summer market', opens daily in summer with stalls selling traditional handicrafts and modern art and crafts. ❸ Esplanada de Cervantes

◐ *Dénia port*

A third hiking route follows the coastline to the Torre del Gerro, an old watchtower above Les Rotes, a fairly easy, one- to two-hour walk. Les Rotes is noted for its excellent fish restaurants. There is also an old English cemetery there.

BEACHES

Dénia has nearly 12 km (7.5 miles) of coastline, with wide, sandy beaches and rocky coastal cliffs. There are long stretches of sandy beach to either side of the port. Sailing, windsurfing, diving and fishing are all on offer for watersports lovers.

If you are here in July, do not miss Bous a la Mar (Bulls at the Sea), part of Dénia's Santísima Sangre fiesta. A bullring is set up along the seaside, and spectators watch the local boys enticing the bulls to chase them into the sea. The afternoon show is free.

RESTAURANTS & BARS (see map on page 58)

Bar Restaurante Pedro €–€€ ❶ Terraced bar restaurant close to the port. Sit outside and watch the world go by while taking coffee or dining on local specialities of grilled meat, fish and *cocas*. ⓐ Pare Pere 3 ☎ 96 575 6432 🕒 Closed Sun

Betibo (Betty Boop) €€ ❷ Lovely open-air bar with easy-on-the-ear music. ⓐ 3 km (1.8 miles) out of town at the bottom of the Dénia–Jávea road 🕒 Only open July and Aug

Bona Plaja €€ ❸ This fish restaurant is right on the beach, good for a cool beer or lunch. In the evening there is flamenco or other entertainment. *Arroz negro* (black rice with calamares) is a speciality, or you can have a steak. ⓐ 3 km (1.8 miles) out of Dénia (look for the signs) on Carretera Las Marinas, Playa las Marinas ☎ 96 578 2777

Mi Villa €€ ❹ This friendly café is clean and bright and a great place to linger over a *horchata* (cold drink made from tiger nuts), milkshake or ice cream while watching local life unfold along this busy shopping street. ⓐ Marqués de Campo 1 ☎ 96 643 0519

El Poblet €€€ ❺ Dine outside on the cool terrace at one of the Costa Blanca's best restaurants. Denia is famous for its prawns, and here they are expertly prepared with other fresh seafood and creative variations on traditional rice dishes. ⓐ Carretera Las Marinas km 2.5 ☎ 96 578 4179 🕒 Closed Sun evening and Mon

Restaurante Tasca Eulalia €–€€ ❻ This is what Spanish food is all about. A *tasca* is an eating house that serves the traditional Spanish tapas, small servings of fish, meat or vegetables, as a gourmet delight to accompany a glass of wine or beer, or a larger portion (*ración*) to add to your table. Full of atmosphere and very popular with the locals. ⓐ Marques de Campo 43 ☎ 96 578 6479

Jalón Valley Vineyards
regional wine centre

The Jalón Valley is the vineyard of the Costa Blanca. Each year growers produce 2.5 million litres (550,000 gallons) of wine. A local cooperative can be found in the village centre of Jalón where you can sample the wines – a red wine similar to claret and the sweet, potent muscatel for which the region is famed – and purchase some at low prices. You can also stop by for tastings at individual *bodegas* (wine cellars) – and fill up your bottle for a song or try some at any bar.

The gentle scenery of the Jalón Valley makes for a pleasant drive. Lush grapevines cover the fields, and you may spot some *riu-raus*, the traditional arched porches used for drying grapes to make raisins. The valley also has a wealth of almond trees, and the many varieties of almond cakes and biscuits are another temptation to indulge.

Almonds, grapes & raisins

Jalón (Xaló) lies at the centre of the valley, a quiet town surrounding a huge church with a shiny silver dome. As far back as 1472, its residents sent their wines to the court of Valencia and began selling a new product that became an economic staple of the Marina Alta: raisins. Look out for the bakery called **La Vicentica**, which turns out tasty fresh bread and cakes – a good place to try the *cocas* (pizzas) and pastries typical of the area. Nearby are the pleasant agricultural villages of Llíber and Alcalalí, with main crops of grapes, oranges and almonds. Parcent was home to Spanish writer Gabriel Miró, who called his town 'a paradise between mountains'.

Fabulous views

From Parcent, follow the road into the mountains towards Tárbena and Callosa to reach the Coll de Rates (Rat's Tail Pass). This is one of the finest viewpoints on the Costa Blanca, with a panorama that sweeps across the Jalón Valley to Dénia, Jávea and the sea.

For more heady views, carry on towards Tárbena through spectacular mountain scenery. The town is surrounded by fruit trees, full of blossoms in the spring, and has a pretty parish church. Beyond the village at the top of the pass is another fantastic viewpoint looking across the peaks and valleys to the coastal high-rises of Benidorm.

 You may want to try some of the area's famous *sobrasadas* (red) or *butifarres* (black) sausages, made to an ancient recipe.

Gata de Gorgos

Near the Jalón Valley, about 9 km (5.5 miles) from Jávea, Gata de Gorgos is known for its wickerwork industry and you will find shops selling baskets, hats, cane furniture and other crafts. Near the train station is a guitar factory where you can see how guitars are made, and buy one at factory prices. ⓐ Guitarras de CashiMira, Calle Estación 25 ⓣ 96 575 6320 ⓛ Open Mon–Fri 09.00–13.00 and 15.00–18.30

RESTAURANTS

El Corral del Pato €€–€€€ Meat *a la brasa* (grilled) is the speciality of this family-run restaurant in the countryside. Enjoy dishes such as duck with fruit or oven-braised lamb (best to order this in advance), accompanied by side dishes typical of the Marina Alta. ⓐ Just on the outskirts of Gata, on the road to Jalón ⓣ 96 575 6834 ⓛ Closed Mon

Casa Parra €€ Friendly restaurant which offers excellent Valencian cuisine served in the small dining room or out on the terrace. Special dishes such as *cordero al horno* (baked lamb) can be ordered in advance and are well worth it. ⓐ Avenida Marina Alta 86, Gata de Gorgos ⓣ 96 575 6121 ⓛ Open 13.00–15.30 and 20.00–23.00

🔽 *Vines in the Jalón Valley*

Benissa
Moorish-style architecture

Benissa, a traditional inland town, is easily reached from Calpe or Moraira. Its quaint Old Town centre has retained its medieval and Moorish architecture and is a lovely place to wander.

Tourist Information Office ❷ Avenida País Valencia 1, at the lower end of town on the N332 towards Valencia. ❶ 96 573 2225 ❶ Open Mon–Sat 09.30–14.00 and 15.00–20.00 (closes earlier in winter), Sun 09.30–14.00. **Parking** There is parking all around Plaza Jaume 1, the central square in Benissa. Make sure you buy a ticket from the machines – the traffic wardens are very vigilant.

WALKING TOUR

Start in Plaza del Portal by the Town Hall, where there is a map showing historic points of interest. The road alongside the Town Hall leads to Plaza Esglesia Vella, a beautiful tiled square with ceramic murals. Walk up the Calle Puríssima, where the medieval houses have Moorish-style tiled porches and *rejas* (iron grilles) over the windows, a protection against pirate attack. Do not miss the ceramic tiles that line the window sills and decorate the undersides of the balconies. You will soon pass the 15th-century Lonja, the old grain and silk exchange with its pretty arched facade. It is now a centre for changing exhibitions on history and culture.

A little further along is another stately building, the 18th-century Casa Torres-Orduña, now the municipal cultural centre and library. Retracing your steps slightly, turn left up Calle Angel to the charming Calle Desamparados, a row of elegant medieval houses with family coats of arms, huge wooden doors and enough wrought iron to withstand the most determined pirates. Carry on up Calle Sant Tómas and Calle Santo Domingo to reach the **Convento de la Puríssima Concepción**,

❶ *A typically narrow street in Benissa*

built in 1612 as a Franciscan monastery. In front is a pretty courtyard ringed with tiled Stations of the Cross. Ring the bell and the custodian will show you around the cloister, chapel and quirky little museum full of fossils, coins, stuffed birds, vestments and artefacts brought back by missionaries from around the world. 🕐 10.00–12.30 and 16.00–18.00

Walk back along Calle San José and Calle San Nicolas to Plaza Jaume 1, for a look at the huge white limestone **Cathedral of the Marina Alta**, which was built between 1902 and 1929. 🕐 Open for visits 11.00–noon only

Then take a well-earned rest and have a drink at one of the bars around the palm tree-shaded square – the friendly **L'Orxatería** (€) serves a tempting array of ice creams and deliciously refreshing *limón granizado*, lemon-flavoured crushed ice. 📞 96 573 1947

BEACHES

Although Benissa is an inland town there are 4 km (2.5 miles) of nearby coastline, stretching between Moraira and Calpe, that contains tranquil coves backed by high cliffs. The biggest and most popular is sandy La Fustera, which is a Blue Flag beach. The Platgeta de L'Advocat has a small marina, which is popular for fishing.

Benissa is known for its rich handmade sausages. Look out for *morcilla*, a type of black pudding, *blancos*, white pork sausages, or *longaniza*, long pork sausages.

FIESTAS

Benissa fiestas start early on in the year, beginning with the three-week-long *Fira i Porrat de San Antoni*, a craft fair held in the streets of the Old Town in January. The fourth Sunday in April is dedicated to the town's patron saint, la Puríssima Xiqueta, with street parties and fireworks. The Moors and Christians take to the streets in the last week of June with mock battles, parades and bands.

◓ *Old Town square, Altea*

Altea
the region's biggest market

The Tuesday morning market in Altea is the biggest on the Costa Blanca. It snakes along the waterfront under a canopy of stalls selling shoes, boots, leather goods, lace and embroidery, clothes, jewellery and assorted goods. Do not expect to find too many local handicrafts, though. You can get there by tour coach, under your own steam or by public transport.

Altea's Old Town is a steep upwards climb of over 200 steps from the waterfront, and you would be hard-pressed to combine it with an excursion to the market unless you are extremely fit and adventurous.

However, this picturesque village is a delightful place for strolling, and merits a separate visit. At the summit is Plaza de la Iglesia. The parish church is crowned by one of the finest blue domes in the region. The sloping streets of immaculate whitewashed houses fan out like bicycle spokes, opening up sparkling views out across the tiled roofs to the sea. There are many restaurants, several *café terrazas* around the large church square and numerous small art galleries in the side streets.

THINGS TO SEE & DO
Palau Altea Centre d'Arts
Altea's exciting new cultural venue linked to the University of Miguel Hernandez. Ongoing exhibitions of the loaned works of famous artists, international theatre groups and nightly music concerts by Europe's finest soloists. Programme information ☎ 96 688 1924
ⓦ www.palaualtea.com

RESTAURANTS
La Capella Bar-Restaurant €–€€ A passageway beside the church leads under a vine-covered arched trellis to a garden patio with a beautiful mountain view. Dishes served up by this traditional kitchen include sausages, paella, seafood, chicken and veal. ⓐ Calle San Pablo 1 ☎ 96 688 0484

El Patio €€ On hot summer days and nights, there is no better place to enjoy Valencian specialities than El Patio's breezy, shaded garden. Fresh grilled fish is always on the menu, along with traditional dishes such as *arroz a la banda*, paella and *fideuá* (paella made with noodles instead of rice). ⓐ Avenida del Puerto 9 ☎ 96 584 3989
🕒 Open March–Oct, closed Thurs

Restaurante Dels Artistes €–€€ Watch the world go by from the large terrace overlooking Plaza de la Iglesia. Food ranges from simple pizzas and pastas to seafood and *zarzuela* (fish and seafood stew). ⓐ Plaza de la Iglesia ☎ 96 584 4279

Guadalest
clifftop stronghold

Guadalest, perched on a rocky outcrop over 610 m (2000 ft) high, is the most visited village on the Costa Blanca. Its white bell tower at the top of a slender granite mass is one of the region's most striking images. Crowned by the ruins of an old Arab fortress, Guadalest was built as a Moorish stronghold during the 8th century. The only access is through a tunnel in the rock, which is why the village remained unconquered.

⬤ *Guadalest bell tower*

The town lies both inside and outside the natural fortress. To reach the castle, its highest point, you must go through the Casa de Orduña. The path winds up to the Castle Square and village cemetery. Parts of the castle were destroyed in the earthquake of 1644. On the streets below, the village square, with its statue of St Gregory (the town's patron) overlooks the aquamarine waters of the reservoir.

Although the crowds of visitors can make Guadalest seem like a theme park, nearly 200 people actually live in this picturesque village. During the day the cobbled streets become a sort of Arab bazaar selling souvenirs and local crafts. The women of the village make elegant shawls, ponchos, lace and embroidered goods. There are several curio museums for amusement, and a number of restaurants.

Bring your camera and plenty of film (or make sure your battery is fully charged if using a digital camera). The drive through the Guadalest Valley is splendid, with terraced slopes of almond, olive and citrus groves giving way to pine forests. Guadalest is featured on many organized tours and excursions – ask your resort representative for details.

SHOPPING

Calle la Virgen, the road where the Museo Belén is situated, is lined with souvenir shops.

Casa Artesana Sells a wide range of craft gifts from more expensive cotton tablecloths and tea sets to tiny eggcups, ceramic bowls and onion jars for a few hundred pesetas. ⓐ Calle la Virgen 4 ⓣ 96 588 5239

Casa de la Miel Offers a huge selection of locally produced honey, as well as brandies, nuts, honey soap and cosmetics. ⓐ At the far end of Calle la Virgen ⓣ 96 588 5258

Regalos Levante This unusual, if pricey, gift shop sells everything from ET tables and models of Captain Hook to more easily transported ceramics, candlesticks, jewellery and scented oil lamps. ⓐ Plaza San Gregorio, at the exit to the castle ⓣ 96 588 5327

THINGS TO SEE & DO

El Arca de Noe ★★★

Do not be put off by the rough road: this animal park, set on a ridge overlooking the Guadalest Valley, carries an overwhelming 'wow' factor for children and adults alike. Its purpose is to rescue wild animals from poor conditions such as circuses and ill-equipped zoos. There is an enormous variety, including a cross-eyed jaguar, pythons with bronchitis, albino deer, anteaters confiscated at customs at Alicante Airport, as well as Phillip the Lion who now roams the mountainside (behind a fence!) after years of living in a 3 by 3 m (10 by 10 ft) cage in a travelling circus. ➌ Near the main Guadalest car park towards Benimantell ➊ 96 597 2359 ➌ Open 10.00–18.00. ➊ Relies on visitors' donations.

Casa de Orduña and castle ★★

This grand mansion was built after the 1644 earthquake by the Orduña family, state governors and guardians of the fortress. Its fine furnishings and artworks reflect the lifestyle of wealthy Spanish aristocrats of the 18th and 19th centuries. ➋ Calle Iglesia 2 ➊ 96 588 5393 ➌ Open 10.15–20.00 (summer); 10.15–13.45 and 15.15–20.00 (winter) ➊ Admission charge

Casa Típica and Ethnological Museum ★

Traditional village life is portrayed in this house museum with antique household implements and tools for producing flour, wine and olive oil. ➊ Calle Iglesia 1 ➊ 96 588 5238 ➌ Open Sun–Fri 10.00–21.00 (summer); 10.00–18.00 (winter) ➊ Admission charge

Fonts de l'Algar ★★

The sparkling rockpools and waterfalls of the Fonts de l'Algar are a refreshing natural oasis formed by a tributary of the Guadalest River. In a lush valley filled with lemon trees and orange groves outside Callosa d'En Sarrià, the river alternates between cascades and clear pools, its banks lined with fragrant summer flowers. You can walk around the trail, pausing for a dip in the icy waters beneath the falls,

before popping into the little environmental museum which shows how essential oils are obtained from plants for use in aromatherapy. ⓐ 3 km/2 miles from Callosa ❶ Admission charge.

In need of refreshment? The Restaurante El Algar de Don Joan (€€) specializes in paella and meat dishes, and you can hang out at the lovely big pool for free. ❶ 96 588 0491. A little further down, the same applies at Casa Marcos (pool open from 11.00 to 20.00 hours).

Young children will enjoy the Museo del Tren, a small museum containing a large model landscape punctuated by miniature trains roaring past the tiny houses, windmills and stations. ⓐ Next to Restaurante El Algar de Don Joan ❶ 96 588 0491 ❶ Open May–Sept 10.30–13.00 and 17.00–21.00 ❶ Admission charge

Museo Belén/Museo de Antonio Marco (Town of Bethlehem Museum) ★★

Exhibits scale models of Spanish architecture and miniature dolls' houses, constructed over 15 years using authentic materials. ⓐ Calle la Virgen 2 ❶ 96 588 5323 ❶ Open 10.00–21.00 (summer); 10.00–18.00 (winter) ❶ Admission charge

Museo de Microminiaturas/Museo Microgigante ★

Two museums, one in Old Town, one near the car park, reveal incredible creations such as an ant playing a violin and famous artworks painted on a grain of rice.
Museo de Microminiaturas ⓐ Calle Iglesia 5 ❶ 96 588 5062.
Museo Microgigante ⓐ Calle del Sol 2 ❶ 96 588 5062 ❶ Both open 10.00–21.00 (summer); 10.00–18.00 (winter) ❶ Admission charge

Museo Moros y Cristianos ★ (Moors and Christians Museum)

The best of the brightly coloured silks, elaborate headgear and sequinned costumes of the annual Moors and Christians festivals are displayed here, along with a history and photographs of these important fiestas. ⓐ 1.5 km (1 mile) before Guadalest on the Callosa d'En Sarrià road ❶ 96 588 5322 ❶ Open 10.00–19.00 ❶ Admission charge

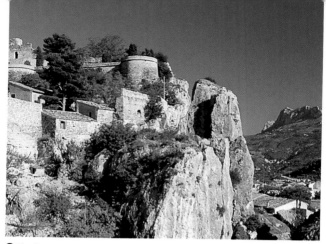

△ *The fortress ruins of Guadalest*

Historical Medieval Museum ★
A gruesome display of instruments of torture and capital punishment.
ⓐ Calle Honda 2 ❶ 96 588 5004 🕐 Open 10.00–21.00 (summer);
10.00–18.00 (winter) ❶ Admission charge

The tourist office is opposite the main entrance to the village
ⓐ Avenida Alicante ❶ 96 588 5298 🕐 Open 11.00–14.00 and
15.00–19.00, closed Sat

RESTAURANTS
Cafetería Levante €–€€ Pop in here for a sandwich, coffee and
cake, or a light lunch of the omelette, salad and chips variety.
ⓐ Plaza San Gregorio 7 ❶ 96 588 5224

L'Hort €€–€€€ This friendly, efficient restaurant serves
high-quality, appetizing food (including a couple of *menús del
día*) on a pretty terrace with a wonderful view over the valley and
mountains beyond. ⓐ Calle la Virgen 1 ❶ 96 588 5269 🕐 Open
12.30–16.30

EXCURSIONS

Alicante
gateway to the Costa Blanca

Alicante, the provincial capital and gateway to the Costa Blanca, deserves more than a visit to the airport. Try and find some time during your holiday to take a tour of this dynamic and historic city.

Iberians, Greeks and Romans had settlements at Alicante. The present city was built by the Moors in the 8th century. It flourished during medieval times, becoming the third-largest seaport in Spain. Alicante has other beaches, museums and monasteries beyond those listed here.

 Tourist office: Avda Rambla de Méndez Núñez 23 ☏ 96 520 0000; Alicante Airport ☏ 96 691 9100; Portugal 17, Bajo ☏ 96 592 9802

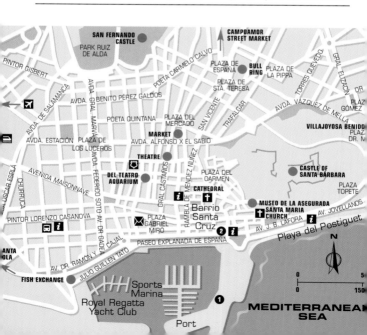

● *Explanada de España*

THINGS TO SEE & DO
Barrio Santa Cruz ★★
The narrow streets of Alicante's old Moorish *barrio* (quarter) provide
a glimpse of Spanish life away from the beach bars. Santa Cruz is a
crumbling maze of roof terraces and flower-filled balconies with
washing flapping in the breeze while women natter on doorsteps.
Everywhere you turn you catch glimpses of glittering fountains tucked
away in pretty squares.

Castle of Santa Bárbara ★★
This 16th-century military fort, built by King Philip II, is perched like a
giant eagle's nest 180 m (590 ft) above the city. There are magnificent
views of the town, beach and bay from several levels – don't forget your
camera. There is also a small museum of ancient artefacts and pottery
and a new exhibition of paintings, sculpture and photography from the
collection of the Institut Valencia d'Art Modern. It is a long, hot walk
up to the castle – to save your legs, you can take a lift up (and down)
from the end of Avenida J.B. Lafora (look for a tunnel entrance cut into
the wall). ● Open 10.00–20.00 (summer); 09.00–19.00 (winter)
❶ Entrance to the castle is free, but there is a moderate charge for
the lift

Explanada de España ★★

Alicante's waterfront promenade is one of the most beautiful in Spain. The broad path of wavy, coloured tiles runs between towering palms, making for a shady place from which to observe Spanish city life over a coffee or an ice cream.

Museo de la Asegurada (Museum of 20th-century Art) ★★

This spacious museum is a pleasure to visit, with enough works by famous artists such as Joan Miró, Max Ernst, Pablo Picasso, Salvador Dalí and Marc Chagall to make it a worthwhile trip for anyone with even a passing interest in modern art. ③ Plaza de Santa María 3 ❶ 96 514 0959 ❶ Open Tues–Sat 10.00–14.00 and 16.00–21.00 (summer); 16.00–20.00 (winter); Sun 10.30–14.30 (all year) ❶ Admission free

SHOPPING

El Corte Inglés Open continuously from 10.00 to 21.30 hours, this spacious department store is a joy to shop in, with everything from quality fashions to homewares and great air-con. Restaurant and toilets are on the top floor. ③ Calle Maisonnave

Markets:
- Alicante's local market. ③ Plaza Campoamor (near the bull-ring) ❶ Thursday and Saturday mornings
- Central Market's mosaic-fronted food market is great to wander through, just to see all the shiny, sun-ripened produce on offer. ③ Avenida de Alfonso X El Sabio ❶ Open Mon–Sat on mornings only

Artesania Reasonably priced ceramics in modern and traditional designs – pick up a pot for *ajos* (garlic) or *arroz* (rice) or splash out on beautiful bowls and cruet sets. ③ Avenida Alfonso X El Sabio 15 ❶ 96 514 0139 ❶ Closed Sat afternoon and Sun

Playa del Postiguet ★★

If you are in need of a cool down, the sandy Playa del Postiguet beach is within easy reach of the town.

 The most secure parking in Alicante is in the attended parking enclosure on Explanada de España opposite the Marina. Shoppers can also use the underground car park of El Corte Inglés department store. Shop until you drop or take the pleasant ten-minute walk through the pretty Parque de Canalejas to the Explanada.

RESTAURANTS (see map on page 76)

La Darsena €€–€€€ ❶ Set alongside the marina and shaped like a ship, this smart restaurant specializes in over 200 kinds of rice dishes. Fresh seafood here is also superb. ➋ Marina Deportiva, Puerto Muelle de Levante ☎ 96 520 7589 🕑 Closed Sun evenings

Peret €€ ❷ This long-established terrace café is the perfect place to indulge in an ice cream, milkshake or traditional *horchata* (cold drink made from tiger nuts). ➋ Explanada de España 1

Alicante's Hogueras de San Juan in the last week of June is one of the region's most famous fiestas; a week-long celebration of summer, with fireworks, parades, all-night parties, live music and bullfights culminating in the Nit del Foc (Night of Fire), when bonfires burn throughout the city.

NIGHTLIFE

The Paseo Marítimo, Alicante's portside promenade, is great for summer-time entertainment. From mid-July to the end of August, there is an international festival of music, dance and theatre including jazz, ballet, symphony orchestras and opera, all in the open air. As well as the shows, the port is a focal point for lively restaurants and bars such as the Irish pub **O'Hara's**, **Nuevo Hong Kong Chinese** and **Popeye's Pizzeria**. The bars in the Barrio Santa Cruz east of the cathedral also come alive at night.

Elche
palm trees and medieval festivals

A former Roman colony, Elche boasts the largest palm grove in Europe with over 300,000 palm trees in and around the city, which are protected by law. Situated on the banks of the Vinalopó River, it is home to over 200,000 inhabitants, although holidaymakers will want to concentrate their attentions on the Old Town, which has plenty of interesting museums and historical buildings to dip in and out of and a myriad of palm tree-shaded squares.

Elche is the centre of Spain's shoemaking industry. Ask at the tourist office on the edge of the Parque Municipal (❶ 96 545 2747) about factories that offer guided tours and the chance to buy shoes at factory prices. ❹ Open Mon–Fri 10.00–19.00, Sat 10.00–14.30, Sun 10.00–14.00

THINGS TO SEE & DO
Baños Arabes ★
The remains of the Arab baths underneath the convent date back to the 12th century, when they were used by the Muslims to purify their bodies before prayer. The baths were closed in 1270, when a convent was established here after the arrival of Christian conquerors, and were later used for storage. A short soundtrack in English explaining the history is available on request. ❸ Convento de la Mercé, Plaça de la Mercé. ❶ 96 545 2887 ❹ Open Tues–Sat 10.00–13.30 and 16.30–20.00, Sun 10.30–13.30 ❶ Admission free

Basilica de Santa María ★
The 17th-century basilica with its blue-tiled dome is the focal point of Elche's Old Town. The inside is very elaborate – take a look at the ornate ceiling where a hatch allows participants in the mystery play (see Fiestas, opposite) to appear from the sky. ❸ Plaça Santa María ❶ 96 545 1540 ❹ Open 11.00–18.00 ❶ Admission free

Huerto del Cura ★★

This glorious garden is filled with the palm trees that made Elche famous. It is a lovely place, dotted with cacti, terrapin and goldfish ponds and beautiful flowers. Look out for the unusual imperial palm with eight palm trees growing from a single stem. There is also a copy of the *Dama de Elche*, which is the symbol of Elche, the bust of a woman that was discovered at La Alcudía, 2 km (1.25 miles) south of Elche, in 1897. A shop sells Elche's specialities, fresh dates and figs, as well as drinks and palm-frond basketwork. ⓐ Porta de la Morera 49 ⓣ 96 545 1936 ⓛ Open 09.00–20.30 (summer); 09.00–18.30 (winter) ⓘ Admission charge

Museo Arqueológico ★

Situated in a former military fortress, this archaeological museum holds a collection of local pottery, statuary and ceramics – the highlights are the 2nd-century *Sleeping Eros* and the headless *Venus de Ilice* from Roman times. ⓐ Palacio de Altamira ⓣ 96 545 3603 ⓛ Open Tues–Sat 10.00–13.00 and 16.00–19.00, Sun 10.00–13.00 ⓘ Admission charge

FIESTAS

The most important festival in Elche is the Misteri d'Elx, a medieval religious play portraying the death of the Virgin and her assumption into heaven. It is staged annually in the basilica on 14 and 15 August. Despite the fact that the all-male cast is amateur, the performance is very professional, a colourful drama of singing, music and angels descending from the basilica's ceiling. There is also a special performance of the mystery play during the Festival of Medieval and Renaissance Theatre and Music, which takes place at the end of October/beginning of November in every even-numbered year.

The Diumenge de Rams (Palm Sunday) procession is also a spectacular sight, when the town's inhabitants parade through the streets carrying white palm branches.

Museo Municipal de la Festa ★★

This museum is dedicated to Elche's famous mystery play portraying the death and assumption of the Virgin Mary (see Fiestas, page 81). One room holds posters advertising the play from 1942 onwards as well as two beautiful 19th-century harps.

The focal point of the museum, however, is the audio-visual display about the history and legends surrounding the death of the Virgin and a look behind the scenes at the preparations and technical tricks that allow the play to be performed in Elche's basilica. The audio-visual display knocks the spots off the average tourist video and an English soundtrack is available. ⓐ Calle Mayor de la Vila ① 96 545 3464 ① Open Tues–Sat 10.00–13.15 and 16.30–20.30 (July–Aug 17.00–21.00), Sun 10.00–13.00 ① Admission charge

Río Safari Elche ★★

For those with children, take a 20-minute boat ride around this safari park for close-up views of tigers, giraffes, hippos, monkeys and other furry and feathered friends. There are also seal shows, a reptile house, an aquarium and camel rides, as well as a go-kart track, slides and swings, trampolines and a swimming pool. ⓐ On the Elche–Santa Pola road (C-3317) about 4 km (2.5 miles) before Santa Pola ① Open 10.30–19.00 ① Admission charge

While you are walking around Elche, look out for palm trees with their branches tied together in order to bleach them (the restricted flow of sap causes the branches to die and turn white) so that they can be cut down and distributed throughout Europe to make crosses for Palm Sunday.

RESTAURANT

Cafetería Africa € Take a break from sightseeing in Elche at this pleasant, down-to-earth café opposite the basilica. Despite the pretty location, the fresh, tasty sandwiches and burgers remain reasonably priced.

Orihuela
ornate buildings and dramatic scenery

Once the capital of the area from Murcia to Alicante, Orihuela today is a town untouched by tourism, where the streets are lined with orange trees and shady squares are fringed with ornate palacios and crumbling facades. The elegant churches and buildings bear witness to the town's rich heritage as an affluent university and cathedral city, before Alicante usurped Orihuela's position as regional capital in the 19th century, making it a pleasant place to soak up some Spanish culture.

THINGS TO SEE & DO

Aquopolis ★★

If the children have seen one church too many, pep them up with a visit to the Aquopolis water park on the north-west outskirts of Torrevieja. It contains all the usual kamikaze slides, a wave pool, a slow river ride and water amusements for children (including big children) of all ages. ❶ 96 571 5890 ❷ Open 11.00–19.00 (mid-June–Aug); 11.00–18.00 (until mid-Sept)

Cathedral ★

This magnificent Catalan Gothic cathedral was built on the site of an ancient mosque at the beginning of the 14th century. It contains attractive cloisters, unusual spiral rib vaulting and a museum. The highlight, however, is Velázquez's painting *The Temptation of Saint Thomas*. ❸ Calle Ramón y Cajal ❷ Open Tues–Sat 10.00–13.00 and 17.00–19.00, Sun 10.00–14.00

Pop into the tourist office for a map at Calle Francisco Diez 25 (❶ 96 530 2747) – it is worth going anyway just to admire the gorgeous tiled entrance hall and floor of the Palacio Rubalcava where it is based. ❷ Open Mon–Fri 09.00–14.30

The countryside around Orihuela

Colegio de Santo Domingo ★★

This former Dominican monastery and university is now a private school, but you can ring the bell and wander through the two glorious cloisters – the outstanding Renaissance cloister around a palm-tree garden and the baroque university cloister built 1727–37. Visit the refectory for a look at the 18th-century ornamental frieze made from Manises tiles. ⓐ Calle Adolfo Clavarana 1 ⓛ Open Tues–Fri 10.00–13.30 and 16.00–19.00, Sat 10.00–14.00 and 16.00–19.00, Sun 10.00–14.00 ⓘ Admission free

Golf ★

The coastal area south of Torrevieja is well equipped with golf courses, with **Villamartín** (ⓛ 96 676 5170) inland from the Playa Zenia and Las Ramblas (ⓛ 96 532 2011) and **Campoamor** (ⓛ 96 532 0410) a little south.

Museo Semana Santa (Easter Week Museum) ★

This museum houses the religious processional effigies that are paraded through the streets as part of Easter celebrations. The most interesting one, the she-devil and skeleton by 17th-century sculptor Nicolas de Bussy, is kept in the Museo de San Juan de Dios. ⓐ Calle del Hospital, just before the Centro de la Salud ⓛ Open daily 10.30–13.30, then Mon–Sat 17.00–20.00 (summer); 16.30–19.00 (winter) ⓘ Admission free. The *diablesa*, which is not allowed into churches, is paraded through the streets on Easter Sunday to scare wrong-doers into repenting. ⓐ Calle Ballesteros Villanueva 1 ⓛ Open Mon–Fri 10.00–13.00 and 16.00–18.00, Sat 10.00–13.00 ⓘ Admission free

BEACHES

Although Orihuela lies 30 km (19 miles) inland, its municipal district encompasses 15 km (9 miles) of coastline, which includes several good beaches such as Campoamor and La Zenia. The large, modern seaside town of Torrevieja with its glorious sandy beaches is also within easy reach. A bit further south lies Torre de la Horadada, a wide stretch of golden sand with a little port, beach bars and pedalos for hire. The atmosphere is young and lively, which makes it popular with teenagers.

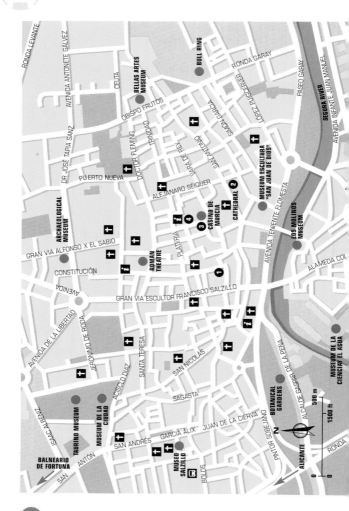

Murcia
beautiful baroque architecture

Murcia is a large city at the heart of the Segura river valley. Surrounded by fertile agricultural land laden with orange orchards, lemon groves and vegetable fields, it was founded by the Moors in the 9th century and has prospered as an agricultural and commercial centre ever since. The city of Murcia itself is a delightful combination of flamboyant baroque architecture, picturesque squares and a medieval old quarter, yet it has enough modern shops to keep the most determined bargain hunter happy.

There is a regional tourist office at Plaza Julián Romea 4, which has information on the surrounding areas as well as on the city itself. ❶ 90 210 1070 ❷ Open Mon–Fri 09.00–14.00

THINGS TO SEE & DO
Casino de Murcia ★★

A stroll through the faded opulence of this casino, built between 1847 and 1901, is like stepping back in time. As you enter, you half expect gentlemen with waxed moustaches, fat cigars and smoking jackets to be brandishing cues in the darkly wooded billiard room, or taffeta-clad ladies to exit from the most ornate powder room you will ever see – huge gilt mirrors, a painted ceiling and magnificent upholstery. The elaborate ballroom, with chandeliers of French crystal, sumptuous fabrics, gilt and carvings, is worth a look, too, as is the entrance hall, a masterpiece of intricate tile work and decoration. ❸ Calle Trapería 22 ❷ Open 09.30–21.00 ❶ Admission charge

If you are driving, it is a good idea to use the parking of the department store, El Corte Inglés – it is well signposted. The underground car park will keep your vehicle cool and it is only a ten-minute walk to the Old Town.

SHOPPING

 Calle Platería is one of the smartest shopping streets in the Old Town and a good place to look for upmarket fashions. Shops worth checking out include **Spaghetti** for chic women's wear and **Ylos** for reasonably priced clothes for the trendy, as well as **Carla** for handbags ranging from the dainty, hand-embroidered evening purse to the functional everyday variety.

Murcia's market takes place around Avenida La Fama, near the General Hospital to the east of the city on Thursday mornings. The Gran Vía Salzillo, the main road leading to the river west of the Old Town, is well equipped with mainstream shops, including the large department store **El Corte Inglés**, **Cortefiel** for good-quality men's and women's wear, and **Bershka** for up-to-the-minute teenage clothes.

Cathedral ★

Murcia's grand cathedral, begun in 1394, encompasses a variety of styles, with a strong Gothic influence inside and baroque curves, carvings and pillars adorning the facade outside. The cathedral museum contains a wood-carving of San Jeronimo holding a cross and a skull by Murcia's most famous son, Francisco Salzillo. ⓐ Plaza Hernández Amores ⓛ Open 10.00–13.00 and 17.00–19.00 (20.00 in summer) ⓘ Admission free, charge for the museum

Museo Salzillo ★

This museum houses the religious sculptures of Murcia-born Francisco Salzillo (1707–83), Spain's most famous 18th-century sculptor. Set out in a beautifully frescoed chapel, nine groups of huge, carved figures depict biblical scenes, which form an important part of the Easter Week celebrations. ⓐ Plaza San Agustín 3 ⓣ 96 829 1893 ⓛ Open Tues–Sat 09.30–13.00 and 16.00–19.00, Sun 11.00–13.00 (Mon–Fri only in July–Aug) ⓘ Admission charge

The Museo Salzillo is a good 20-minute walk from the cathedral – on a hot day, it is worth flagging down a taxi.

Balneario de Fortuna ★

If it is too hot to be tramping around museums and monuments, then indulge in the little spa village of Balneario de Fortuna, 25 km (15.5 miles) north-west of Murcia. At one of the three Balneario de Fortuna hotels, you can relax with a thermal massage or soak in a spa bubble bath at affordable prices. Treatments are available mornings only, 08.00–13.00 hours, and it is best to book (🕿 96 868 5011). There is also a wonderful outdoor swimming pool where you can spend the day. 🕒 Open 10.00–21.00 (summer); 10.00–17.00 (winter) ❶ Admission charge

RESTAURANTS & BARS (see map on page 86)

 La Abadía de San Antonio €€ ❶ Lovely traditional tapas bar in an attractive arched building. ⓐ Calle Sociedad 1 🕿 96 821 1091

Mesón El Corral de José Luis €€ ❷ Indulge in a variety of tapas, from fresh anchovies and squid to stuffed peppers, artichokes and mushroom kebabs in this beautifully tiled authentic Spanish restaurant, or choose a Murcian speciality from their extensive à la carte menu. ⓐ Plaza Santo Domingo 🕿 96 821 4597

Raimundo González €€ ❸ Have lunch with a little luxury under the chandeliers in the grand dining room at the Casino. Despite the formal setting and bow-tied waiters, the set menu will not cost you the earth. ⓐ Casino de Murcia, Calle Trapería 22 🕿 96 822 0658 🕒 Open for lunch only, 13.30–16.30, closed Mon

Romcón de Pepe €€–€€€ ❹ Two excellent options in Murcia's smartest hotel: a superb selection of tapas is served in La Muralla tapas bar, built around a part of an ancient Arabic wall. The elegant formal restaurant serves superb grilled meats, fresh seafood and regional dishes. ⓐ NH Rincón de Pepe, Calle Apóstoles 🕿 96 821 2239

Cartagena
modernist buildings and lively Old Quarter

Cartagena was founded by the Carthaginians in 227 BC before spending several centuries under Roman domination. The city's location around a natural harbour, combined with the riches from the surrounding silver mines, made it a highly prized possession. Nowadays it is a mixture of modern industrial city, naval dockyards and a very attractive *casco antiguo* (old quarter), which is a blend of Roman ruins, elegant churches and some wonderful modernist buildings.

THINGS TO SEE & DO
Calle Mayor ★ ★

If you are in Cartagena for the evening, join the throng of locals in the ritual pre-dinner stroll up and down this street, browse the shop windows, and stop off for an ice cream or aperitif at one of the many bars or cafés.

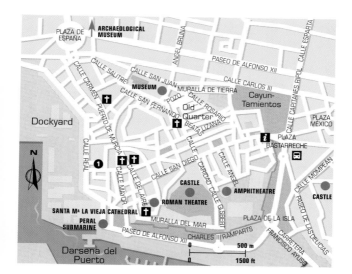

Old Quarter ★★

Stroll through the Old Quarter to admire the marvellous facades of the modernist buildings. Look out for the **Palacio de Aguirre** on the corner of Plaza Merced with its shiny domed tower and rococo ceramic motifs – the bees on the tower signify diligence and industry. The Gaudí-inspired **Maestre House**, now a bank, in Plaza San Francisco has beautiful wrought-iron and stone balconies, and the richly decorated **Llagostera House** in Calle Mayor is also worth a look.

Peral submarine ★

Down by the port is the original model of what Cartagena claims to be the first submarine, built by local inventor Isaac Peral in 1888.

◐ *Cartagena has a fine natural harbour*

Roman theatre ★

This crumbling theatre was built in 3 BC. Nearby is the ruined, 13th-century Cathedral of Santa María. Bombarded during the Spanish Civil War, there are now plans to restore it. ❷ Calle Soledad

---

The tourist office at Puertas San José (❶ 96 850 6483) can supply a map of all the modernist buildings in Cartagena.

RESTAURANTS (see map on page 91)

A cluster of traditional Spanish restaurants in Plaza del Rey ❶ offer excellent tapas and good-value *menús del día* under flower-covered canopies overlooking the square. **La Cazuela** at no. 3 (❶ 96 850 0700) serves straightforward, tasty dishes including specialities such as vegetarian paella and *sopa de mariscos* (seafood soup) with a fixed-priced menu in the evening as well as at lunchtime. The next-door **Rincón Real** is a great place for tapas.

From around 10 July to the end of the month, there is an ethnic music festival in Parque Torres and Parque Artillería from 23.00 (admission charge). In the same period, you can enjoy a great atmosphere and good music for free – live bands often play at around 20.00 in the Plaza del Ayuntamiento, in front of the Town Hall.

FIESTAS

Cartagena has a programme of festivals throughout the year. In February, there is a lively carnival. Easter Week sees sombre processions and marching bands. One of the most important festivals is the ten-day Carthaginian and Roman fiesta in the second half of September, with mock battles, legions of marching Roman and Carthaginian troops, and fireworks. Both sides set up historical camps, with food and drink to reflect the era, then party the night away to the anachronistic sounds of modern dance music.

LIFESTYLE
The Costa Blanca way

Food & drink

There is fabulous food to try all over the Costa Blanca, and meals are generally good value. Paella is the regional speciality, made of saffron rice prepared with seafood, chicken or vegetables. With fine cava, Spanish champagne (sparkling white wine), so affordable, you will be celebrating every night. The Spanish eat quite late, but in tourist areas you will be able to find places that serve meals throughout the day. Generally, lunch is served from 13.00 to 15.00 or 16.00 and dinner from around 19.30 until 23.00 or midnight.

LIGHT LUNCHES & SNACKS

If you just want a sandwich, ask for a *bocadillo*, which is usually a hearty baguette made with tasty *serrano* ham, cheese and other fillings. *Cocas* are pies or mini pizzas, popular all over this region. They consist of a shortcrust pastry with various ingredients. A favourite is made with tuna fish, tomatoes and onions and looks like a Cornish pasty. There are also plenty of Western-style fast food outlets and cafés that serve sandwiches and snacks.

TAPAS

These snacks were traditionally served as 'a little something' to accompany wine or sherry. They can range from nuts or olives to tasty morsels of ham and cheese, croquettes, squid or sardines. A selection of tapas makes a lovely light lunch. You can also ask for larger portions, called *raciones*.

RICE

Rice is the regional dish of Valencia province, prepared in countless variations in every town on the Costa Blanca. The most famous is *paella valenciana*, saffron rice with chicken and vegetables. Paellas are also made with fish, seafood and rabbit. Try *arroz negro*, a paella made with *calamares* (squid) and rice turned black from the squid's ink. *Arroz a banda* and *caldero* are rice dishes made with fish stock.

MEATS

Look out for barbecue restaurants that do meat *a la brasa* – cooked on a brazier. Choose from savoury pork chops, steaks or lamb cutlets. Other meats are prepared with delicious flavourings. Try *conejo al ajillo* (rabbit simmered in oil and garlic).

Sausages are particularly excellent, and some Costa Blanca towns are famed for their secret recipes, some of them very old. *Butifarres* are white and black puddings made with either meat or onions. The red *sobrasadas* are seasoned with aromatic herbs from the mountains.

⬤ *Paella: a local speciality*

If you are renting an apartment or villa, look for takeaway paella. Served in the paella pan, as in a restaurant, you pay a deposit to ensure the pan's return the next day. Spaniards eat paella for the midday meal, although most restaurants serve it in the evening. It is made to order and takes at least 30 minutes to prepare. The price is per person (minimum two people).

SEAFOOD

Seafood abounds on the Costa Blanca, and much of it is quite reasonably priced. Many fish are caught locally – try grilled red mullet or sardines, sea bass cooked in sea salt or fried baby whiting. *Langostinos* (giant prawns) are especially popular. A regional speciality is *zarzuela*, a kind of seafood stew. *Calamares* (squid) can be cooked in a sauce or is often deep-fried. Squeeze some lemon juice over it.

Another Alicante delicacy is salted fish, such as sardines, tuna, cod and fish roe, accompanied by pickled onions, capers and olives – a substantial aperitif.

TYPICAL DISHES TO TRY

- **Albondigas** Meatballs, usually served as tapas.
- **Alioli** Spread this thick garlic mayonnaise on toasted bread.
- **Gazpacho** In effect, liquid salad. Chilled soup made of puréed tomato, onion, cucumber, green pepper and garlic. Refreshing in hot weather.
- **Tortilla Española** (*tortilla de patatas*). Thick Spanish omelette made with potatoes. Served as tapas or in a *bocadillo* (sandwich).

BRITISH

If you're looking for a taste of home, most resorts can offer fish and chips, steak-and-kidney pie, ploughman's lunches and full English breakfasts, all washed down with a cuppa or a British beer.

DESSERTS

Watermelons, figs, pears and strawberries are among summer's cornucopia of fruit. There are delicious pastries, often made with almonds or honey. *Flan* (crème caramel), *helado* (ice cream) and *tarta* (cake) with fruit are also popular.

COFFEE & TEA

Tea is not a Spanish forte, but coffee-lovers are in for a treat. *Café solo* is strong and black, served in a small glass. *Café cortado* is also strong and served with a splash of milk or cream. *Café con leche* comes in a larger cup and is half coffee, half milk. If you find the *café solo* too strong (and too small), ask for *un café americano* – which is a larger version of the *café solo* with extra water added.

🔺 *Eating out in Valencia*

WINES, BEER & SPIRITS

Spain produces excellent wines, beers and spirits, *jerez* (sherries) and *cava* (champagne-style sparkling wine). A good *cava* is Codorníu, and you will also recognize Freixenet, sold at home at twice the price. Both have *brut* (dry) and semi-dry varieties.

The Jalón Valley is famous for its muscatel grape, which produces a sweet, strong dessert wine of the same name.

There are plenty of the popular Rioja wines around, but be sure to try some of Alicante's own excellent *vino tinto* (red). *Viña Vermeta* is nice, with a hint of vanilla. Or visit a *bodega* (wine cellar) in the Jalón Valley, where you can try before you buy. In restaurants you can often order a jug of the *vino de la casa* (house wine).

San Miguel is a good and inexpensive Spanish lager. Spanish brandies are also good value, although they can be a little rough at the lower end of the price scale.

↘ Many restaurants offer a *menú del día* (menu of the day). These can be excellent value – the three-course meal will usually include dessert, wine and bread.

Menu decoder

aceitunas aliñadas Marinated olives

albóndigas en salsa Meatballs in (usually tomato) sauce

albóndigas de pescado Fish cakes

alioli Garlic-flavoured mayonnaise served as an accompaniment to just about anything – a rice dish, vegetables, shellfish – or as a dip for bread

bistek or **biftek** Beef steak; **poco hecho** is rare, **regular** is medium and **bien hecho** is well done

bocadillo The Spanish sandwich, usually made with French-style bread

caldereta A stew based on fish or lamb

caldo A soup or broth

carne Meat; **de ternera** is beef, **picada** is minced meat, **de cerdo** is pork and **de cordero** is lamb

chorizo A cured, dry, red-coloured sausage made from chopped pork, paprika, spices, herbs and garlic

churros Flour fritters cooked in spiral shapes in very hot fat and cut into strips, best dunked into hot chocolate

cordero asado Roast lamb flavoured with lemon and white wine

embutidos charcutería Pork meat preparations including **jamón** (ham), **salchichones** (sausages) and **morcillas** (black pudding)

ensalada salad; the normal restaurant salad is composed of lettuce, onion, tomato and olives.

ensalada mixta As above, but with extra ingredients, such as boiled egg, tuna fish or asparagus

escabeche A sauce of fish, meat or vegetables cooked in wine and vinegar and left to go cold

estofado de buey Beef stew, made with carrots and turnips, or with potatoes

fiambre Any type of cold meat such as ham, **chorizo**, etc.

flan Caramel custard, the national dessert of Spain

fritura A fry-up, as in **fritura de pescado** – different kinds of fried fish

gambas Prawns; **a la plancha** is grilled prawns, **al ajillo** is prawns fried with garlic, **gambas con gabardina** is prawns deep-fried in batter

gazpacho andaluz Cold soup (originally from Andalucía) made from tomatoes, cucumbers, peppers, bread, garlic and olive oil

gazpacho manchego A hot dish made with meat (chicken or rabbit) and unleavened bread (not to be confused with **gazpacho andaluz**)

habas con jamón Broad beans fried with diced ham (sometimes with chopped hard-boiled egg and parsley)

helado Ice cream

jamón Ham; **serrano** is dry cured, **iberico** is dry cured but far more expensive, and **de york** is cooked ham

langostinos a la plancha Large prawns grilled and served with vinaigrette or alioli; **langostinos a la marinera** are cooked in white wine

lenguado Sole, often served cooked with wine and mushrooms

mariscos Seafood, including shellfish

menestra A dish of mixed vegetables cooked separately and combined before serving

menú del día Set menu for the day at a fixed price; it may or may not include bread, wine and a dessert, but does not usually include coffee

paella Famous rice dish originally from Valencia but now made all over Spain; **paella valenciana** has chicken and rabbit; **paella de mariscos** is made with seafood; **paella mixta** combines meat and seafood

pan Bread; **pan de molde** is sliced white bread; **pan integral** wholemeal

pincho moruno Pork kebab: spicy chunks of pork on a skewer

pisto The Spanish version of ratatouille, made with tomato, peppers, onions, garlic, courgette and aubergines

pollo al ajillo Chicken fried with garlic; **pollo a la cerveza** is cooked in beer; **pollo al chilindrón** is cooked with peppers, tomatoes and onions

salpicón de mariscos Seafood salad

sopa de ajo Delicious, warming, winter garlic soup, thickened with bread, usually with a poached egg floating in it

tarta helada A popular ice-cream cake served as dessert

tortilla española The classic omelette, made with potatoes and eaten hot or cold; if you want a plain omelette ask for a **tortilla francesa**

zarzuela de pescado y mariscos A stew made with white fish and shellfish in a tomato, wine and saffron stock

🔺 *Try markets for souvenirs*

Shopping

Spain is noted for its leather goods, and Benidorm and Dénia have shops with fine selections of coats, jackets, handbags, wallets, belts, luggage and shoes.

HANDICRAFTS

Lladró handmade porcelain statues and figurines are famous worldwide and are made near the Costa Blanca, on the Costa Azahar. They are on sale throughout the resorts and at the factory outlet store in Valencia (see page 50). Look for lace tablecloths, shawls and crochet work in Guadalest, cane and basketwork in Gata de Gorgos and pottery in Elche.

If you would like to try your hand at making paella when you get home, you can find a paella pan at *ferreterías* (hardware stores) and street markets.

FOOD & DRINK

- **Almonds**, **honey** and **chocolate** are other regional food specialities that are nice to take home.
- **Muscatel** is a very sweet dessert wine made locally in the Costa Blanca region. Spanish *cavas* (sparkling wines) and table wines are bargains, both around the resorts and at the airport.
- **Turrón** is a sweet made of almonds and honey, produced in Jijona, a mountain village. There are many varieties. An inexpensive treat to pick up as a present.

 The large supermarkets are a good place to find good wine at low prices. **Carrefour** hypermarket is located just off the Benidorm bypass. ⏱ Open Mon–Sat 10.00–22.00

MARKETS

Markets are generally held one day a week in towns throughout the Costa Blanca. They open at 08.30 and close at about 14.00. It is easy to find them as they form the focal point of the town on market days, particularly the fruit and vegetable sections. You can go to the markets at Altea and Calpe by tour coach; contact your tourist office for further details.

Markets around the Costa Blanca include:

- Monday   Dénia, Callosa, La Nucia
- Tuesday   Altea
- Wednesday   Benidorm, Cartagena
- Thursday   Villajoyosa, Jávea, Alicante, Murcia
- Friday   L'Alfàs del Pi, Finestrat
- Saturday   Alicante, Calpe
- Sunday   Benidorm, La Nucia car boot sale

Kids

Children are well catered for on the Costa Blanca. There are special excursions for children and families, such as the Castle Conde de Alfaz (see page 32) and there are plenty of playgrounds dotted about. Children are also welcomed in restaurants.

Those beaches that have clean, soft sand and shallow water are particularly good for children. They enjoy exploring the castles at Dénia and Alicante and the boat trips from Benidorm to Calpe or Peacock Island (see page 28).

BENIDORM
Aqualandia ★★★
This thrilling water park is said to be the largest in Europe. Here you can ride the Rapids, take a Kamikaze Slide or venture into the Black Hole. The park is beautifully landscaped into the mountainside, with gardens, waterfalls, fountains, pools, sunbeds and picnic areas providing cool havens. Olympic divers dressed as comic clowns put on two or three shows a day. ❸ Rincón de Loix, Benidorm ❶ 96 586 4006/7/8 Ⓦ www.aqualandia.net ❺ aqualandia@aqualandia.net ◐ Depending on the weather, Aqualandia opens in May and closes in September or October. Hours are 10.00–17.30 or 18.00, and until 19.00 or 19.30 in July and Aug ❶ Admission charge

Mundomar ★★★
Next door to Aqualandia (you can visit both on a combined ticket), the Costa Blanca's 'Seaworld' also has a colourful array of toucans, flamingos, bats and birds. Do not miss the beautiful Guacamayo, a huge blue parrot from Brazil. Dolphins perform twice a day in the dolphinarium, and the parrots and sea lions also put on a show. ❸ Rincón de Loix, Benidorm ❶ 96 586 9101/2/3 Ⓦ www.mundomar.es ❺ mundomar@mundomar.es ◐ Open 10.00–18.00 (Oct–Apr); until 18.30 (May–Sept); until 20.00 (mid-July–Aug) ❶ Admission charge

🔺 *All the fun of the fair*

> For unique souvenirs, visit the gift shop at Mundomar. It has a great selection of ecological T-shirts, stuffed toy turtles and walruses, beautiful baskets, crystal dolphins and wind chimes of wood and shells.

Terra Mítica ★★★
This giant theme park recreates the ancient civilizations of Rome, Greece, Egypt, Iberia and the Barbary Coast (see page 27). The newest attraction is a water-borne journey of the 'Rescue of Ulysses'. ➍ Access from the A-7 (Exit 65-A) and the N-332 at Benidorm, plus regular bus and train services ➊ 90 202 0220 or log onto ⓦ www.terramiticapark.com

Funfairs and trains ★★
The larger resorts have funfairs for younger children with carousels, toy train rides and the like. Children (and their tired parents) will also appreciate the *trenes turísticos* (tourist trains) that tour around many resort areas (see Xátiva, page 56).

Sports & activities

BEACHES

The Costa Blanca is renowned for its crystal-blue water and fine white sands. Beaches are clean and well maintained. Many have been given the Blue Flag mark of excellence, distinguishing them as environmentally sound, first-class tourist beaches. These include:

- **Alicante** San Juan, La Albufereta, Tabarca Island
- **Benidorm** Levante, Poniente and Mal Pas
- **Benissa** Cala Fustera
- **Calpe** La Fossa-Levante, El Arenal-Bol
- **Dénia** Las Marinas, Las Rotas
- **Elche** Los Arenales, El Pinet
- **Finestrat** La Cala
- **Jávea** El Arenal, Las Aduanas del Mar (la Grava)
- **Moraira** El Portet, L'Ampolla
- **Santa Pola** Levante

In addition to the large public beaches, there are small beaches in hidden coves, beaches with dunes, and beaches with pine forests or palm trees; often found down tracks marked '*Playa*' or '*Cala*' off main roads.

 There is little natural shade on most beaches, so be prepared to pay for rented sun umbrellas.

WATER SPORTS

Many different water sports are on offer all along the Costa Blanca. Two main centres are Dénia and Calpe. Dénia has sailing, windsurfing, diving, fishing and rowing. Stop by Calpe's Nautical Club at the port for information on windsurfing, waterskiing, scuba diving and sailing. Sailing courses are available. Jávea also has scuba-diving centres and tuition. In Benidorm, you can learn to water-ski using the Cable Ski system at the Rincón de Loix end of the Levante beach (❶ 96 585 1386). There are also several scuba-diving centres.

GOLF

There are 14 courses on the
Costa Blanca. They are open
year-round and have club and
golf-cart rental. Some of the
best include: Club de Golf Don
Cayo, a 9-hole course in Altea
(❶ 96 584 8046); Club de Golf
Jávea, a 9-hole course on the
main Jávea–Benitachell road
(❶ 96 579 2584); Club de Golf
Ifach, a 9-hole course on the
San Jaime residential estate
on the Moraira–Calpe road
(❶ 96 649 7114/6) and Club
de Golf La Sella, an 18-hole
course near Dénia on the
La Jara–Jesús Pobre road
(❶ 96 645 4252).

◐ *Good walking country*

GO-KARTS

One of the best go-kart tracks lies between Benidorm and Villajoyosa.
🕐 Open 09.00–02.00 (summer); 09.00–dark (winter). There is also a
small track at Jávea.

HIKING

Above Benidorm is the Sierra Helada, which is over 400 m (1312 ft) high
and has the highest coastal cliffs in the whole of the Mediterranean.
There are easy to moderate walking routes from town into the hills and
across the ridge – these have expansive sea views. Ask at the tourist
office for details.

HORSE RIDING

There are stables in La Nucia just outside Benidorm. Guides are available.

Festivals & events
traditional celebrations

You can see the bright frilly skirts and castanets of flamenco performers all around the Costa Blanca. This passionate form of music and dance has Arabic origins and developed in southern Spain. There are two styles. Bars, clubs and restaurants often feature the animated light style, with much hand-clapping, heel-drumming and finger-snapping. True flamenco is the mournful music of hardship that sprang from the mining villages, with the sombre dances passed down from generation to generation. Another regional variation is the *sevillanas*, a happy style of folk music and dance associated with fiestas.

Check out the English newspaper *Costa Blanca News* for tips on local events, activities and restaurants. It comes out once a week on Fridays.

FIESTAS

Spanish culture is celebrated in fiestas throughout the year. Many are religious festivals dedicated to a particular saint and are marked by street processions and church services. Other fiestas involve colourful feasts, fireworks and bull-running, with the celebrations lasting a week or more.

The Costa Blanca's most famous fiesta is the Moors and Christians. It is celebrated in different towns throughout the year, though the finest is said to be at Alcoy on St George's Day (23 April). Townsfolk re-enact the battles of their ancestors; whether you masquerade as a Moor or a Christian is a matter of tradition, which is handed down from generation to generation.

Jávea and Villajoyosa hold their Moors and Christians festival in July, Dénia in August, Altea in September, Benidorm in September/October and Calpe in October.

▶ *Festival in Valencia*

◢ *Traditional Flamenco dancing*

Another spectacular event is the *Fallas* (pronounced fye-yas) fiesta, when, after a week of festivities, giant satirical figures are set alight in the town squares on St Joseph's Day (San José), 19 March. Valencia's Fallas (12–19 March) is one of the biggest fiestas in Spain. Around 370 giant papier-mâché floats, up to 18 m (60 ft) high, take to the streets on the night of 15 March. There is a topical twist to the *ninots* (effigies), which represent politicians, bullfighters, members of the jet set and a whole variety of public figures. The culmination of the celebrations, the Festival of San José, takes place on 19 March, when the *ninots* are set alight, a symbolic burning of the old in order to welcome the spring. Others are held in Calpe, Dénia and Benidorm. A similar event is Hogueras de San Juan (Bonfires of St. John), held in Alicante on 24 June; smaller *hogueras* take place in Jávea, Dénia, Benidorm and Calpe at this time.

Each town celebrates the feast day of its patron. Among the highlights are Dénia's Santísima Sangre fiesta in July, with the exciting Bulls at the Sea event (see page 61) where bulls are enticed to chase locals into the water, Calpe's Virgin of the Snows, on 5–6 August, with floats, parades and a bull-run in the streets and Benidorm's patron saint festivities in November.

> When you see the streets decorated with coloured streamers (bunting), it may mean that they have just had – or will soon have – a fiesta, so look out for posters with details of events.

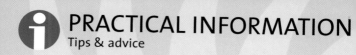

Preparing to go

GETTING THERE

The least expensive way to get to the Costa Blanca is to book a package holiday with one of the leading tour operators specializing in Costa Blanca holidays. You should also check the travel supplements of the weekend newspapers such as the *Sunday Telegraph* and the *Sunday Times*. They often carry adverts for inexpensive flights, as well as classified adverts for privately owned villas and apartments to rent in most popular holiday destinations. If your travelling times are flexible, you can also find some very cheap last-minute deals using the websites for the leading holiday companies.

BY AIR

The Costa Blanca is served by Alicante's main international airport El Altet, 10 km (6 miles) south-west of the city. Some smaller carriers are making increasing use of San Javier Airport in Murcia with flights direct from Stansted. Scheduled flights to Alicante are operated by the Spanish national carrier Iberia Airlines and British Airways. Both airlines offer online flight availability and bookings through their respective websites. ℮ www.iberia.com and www.britishairways.com.

BEFORE YOU LEAVE

Holidays should be about fun and relaxation, so avoid last-minute panics and stress by making your preparations well in advance.

It is not necessary to have inoculations to travel in Europe, but you should make sure you and your family are up to date with the basics, such as tetanus. It is a good idea to pack a small first-aid kit to carry with you. Sun lotion can be expensive in the Costa Blanca so it is worth taking a good selection of the higher factor lotions if you have children with you, and do not forget after-sun cream as well. If you are taking prescription medicines, ensure that you take enough for the duration of your visit – you may find it impossible to obtain the same medicines in the Costa Blanca. It is also worth having a dental check-up before you go.

DOCUMENTS

The most important documents you will need are your tickets and your passport. Check well in advance that your passport is up to date and has at least three months left to run (six months is even better). All children, including newborn babies, need their own passport now, unless they are already included on the passport of the person they are travelling with. It generally takes at least three weeks to process a passport renewal. This can be even longer in the run-up to the summer months. For the latest information on how to renew your passport and the processing times call the **Passport Agency** on 0870 521 0410, or access their website ⓔ www.ukpa.gov.uk. All Spanish nationals and foreign residents are issued with ID cards, which must be produced on demand. You must carry your passport with you at all times when in Spain.

You should check the details of your travel tickets well before your departure, ensuring that the timings and dates are correct.

If you are thinking of hiring a car while you are away, you will need to have your UK driving licence with you. If you want more than one driver for the car, the other drivers must have their licence too.

MONEY

You will need some currency before you go, especially if your flight gets you to your destination at the weekend or late in the day after the banks have closed. Travellers' cheques provide the safest way to carry money because the money will be refunded if the cheques are lost or stolen. To buy travellers' cheques or exchange money at a bank you may need to give up to a week's notice, depending on the quantity of foreign currency you require. You can exchange money at the airport before you depart. You should also make sure that your credit, charge and debit cards are up to date – you do not want them to expire in the middle of your holiday – and that your credit limit is sufficient to allow you to make those holiday purchases. Do not forget, too, to check your PIN numbers in case you have not used them for a while – you may want to draw money from cash dispensers while you are away. Ring your bank or card company and they will help you out.

INSURANCE

Have you got sufficient cover for your holiday? Check that your policy covers you adequately for loss of possessions and valuables, for activities you might want to try – such as scuba-diving, horse-riding, or water sports – and for emergency medical and dental treatment, including flights home if required.

After January 2006, a new EHIC card replaces the E111 form to allow UK visitors access to reduced-cost, and sometimes free state-provided medical treatment in the EEA. For further information, ring EHIC enquiries line: ☎ 0845 605 0707 or visit the Department of Health website Ⓦ www.dh.gov.uk

CLIMATE

Take into account the time of year you are travelling when choosing clothes to take with you. Light casual wear is fine in summer, but you will need at least one warm item for the evenings, when temperatures can drop a few degrees. The Costa Blanca has little summer rainfall, but when it comes it can be heavy – a light plastic raincoat takes up very little room in your suitcase and you may be glad of it if caught in a summer storm. Avoid falling into the 'tourist trap' of taking clothes suitable only for the beach. Many nightclubs and restaurants will refuse bare chests, bikinis and shorts so make sure you pack some smart casual wear for the evenings.

PETS

In some cases you may be able to take your domestic pet abroad with you under the new Pets' Passport Scheme, but there is a lengthy period between inoculation and the issue of a travelling certificate.

TELEPHONING COSTA BLANCA

To call Gran Canaria from the UK, dial 00 34 then the nine-digit number – there's no need to wait for a dialling tone.

SECURITY

Take sensible precautions to prevent your house being burgled while you are away:

- Cancel milk, newspapers and any other regular deliveries you may have so that post and milk do not pile up on your doorstep, indicating that you are away.
- Let the postman know where to leave parcels and bulky items that will not go through your letterbox – ideally with a next-door neighbour.
- If possible, arrange for a friend or neighbour to visit regularly, closing and opening curtains in the evening and morning, and switching lights on and off to give the impression that the house is being lived in while you are away.
- Consider buying electrical devices that will switch lights and radios on and off, to give the impression that there is someone in the house.
- Let Neighbourhood Watch representatives know that you will be away so that they can keep an eye on your home.
- If you have a burglar alarm, make sure that it is serviced and working properly and is switched on when you leave (you may find that your insurance policy requires this). Ensure that a neighbour is able to gain access to the alarm to turn it off if it is set off accidentally.
- If you are leaving cars unattended, put them in a garage, if possible, and leave a key with a neighbour in case the alarm goes off.

AIRPORT PARKING & ACCOMMODATION

If you intend to leave your car in an airport car park while you are away, or stay the night at an airport hotel before or after your flight, you should book well ahead to take advantage of discounts or cheap off-airport parking. Airport accommodation gets booked up several weeks in advance, especially during the height of the holiday season. Check whether the hotel offers free parking for the duration of the holiday – often the savings made on parking costs can significantly reduce the accommodation price.

PACKING TIPS

Baggage allowances vary according to the airline, destination and class of travel, but 20 kg (44 lb) per person is the norm for luggage that is carried in the hold (it usually tells you what the weight limit is on your ticket). You are also permitted a single item of cabin baggage weighing no more than 5 kg (11 lb), and measuring 46 by 30 by 23 cm (18 by 12 by 9 in). In addition, you can usually carry your duty-free purchases, umbrella, handbag, coat, camera, etc., as hand baggage.

● *If you are taking golf clubs, these are charged as extras*

Large items – surfboards, golf-clubs, collapsible wheelchairs and pushchairs – are usually charged as extras and it is a good idea to let the airline know in advance if you want to bring these.

CHECK-IN, PASSPORT CONTROL & CUSTOMS

First-time travellers can find airport security intimidating, but it is all very easy, really.

- Check-in desks usually open 2 or 3 hours before the flight is due to depart. Arrive early for the best choice of seats.
- Look for your flight number on the TV monitors in the check-in area, and find the relevant check-in desk. Your tickets will be checked and your luggage taken. Take your boarding card and go to the departure gate. Here your hand luggage will be X-rayed and your passport checked.
- In the departure area, you can shop and relax, but watch the monitors that tell you when to board – usually about 30 minutes before take-off. Go to the departure gate shown on the monitor and follow the instructions given to you by the airline staff.

During your stay

BEACHES

In summer, many beaches have lifeguards and a flag safety system (see box, below). Observe beach warning flags and never enter the sea when the yellow or red flags are flying. Other beaches may be safe for swimming but there are unlikely to be lifeguards or life-saving amenities available.

Bear in mind that the strong winds that develop in the hotter months can quickly change a safe beach into a not-so-safe one, and some can have strong currents the further out that you go. If in doubt, ask your local representative or at your hotel.

CHILDREN'S ACTIVITIES

The Spanish love children, who seem to wander around until all hours, and provide many activities. Most beaches have dedicated play areas and the Costa Blanca offers a host of attractions including the Terra Mítica theme park (see page 27) and Aqualandia and Mundomar water parks (see pages 24 and 26).

CONSULATE

The Costa Blanca is served by the British Consulate in Alicante City. ⓐ Plaza Calvo Sotelo 1 ⓣ 96 521 6022 and 96 521 6190. An emergency number is provided for calling the Consulate out of hours. ⓛ Open Mon–Thurs 08.00–14.00, Fri 08.30–13.30 (summer).

BEACH SAFETY
Take note of the flag system that advises you of swimming conditions.
- **Green** = safe bathing and swimming for all
- **Yellow** = caution – strong swimmers only
- **Red** = danger – no swimming

CURRENCY

Spain is now in the Euro, with €1 equalling 100 cents. Coins are €1, €2 and 1, 2, 5, 10, 20 and 50 cents. Notes are €5, €10, €20, €50, €100, €200 and €500. Use banks to exchange your pounds or travellers' cheques, rather than street kiosks where you may be charged a high commission fee. Before parting with your money, always ask how much you will receive in return less any commission or expenses.

Banks Open Monday to Friday 09.30–14.00 hours. In winter they may open in the afternoons for short periods and on Saturday mornings. Cashpoint machines are available in the larger resorts, with instructions in English.

Exchange bureaux Opening hours of exchange bureaux are similar to those of shops. Rates of exchange can vary considerably. Note that some quoted rates may be based on the exchange of a minimum amount, and the service charge could be up to two per cent, or a set fee. You may also be able to exchange both cash and travellers' cheques at the reception desk at your hotel.

Credit Cards Upmarket restaurants and department stores take credit cards, as do some of the petrol stations in main resort areas. Shops that accept credit cards will display the signs in their windows. Visa and MasterCard are most widely recognized. You will need cash in smaller restaurants, shops and towns.

ELECTRICITY

Spain operates under the 220V system so all appliances from the UK will work, but you will need a plug-adaptor kit, which you should be able to buy your local high street. Less fiddly is a simple plug that adapts the standard UK 3-pin to the Spanish 2-pin earthed system. These are available in most Spanish hardware shops.

If you are considering buying electrical appliances to take home, always check that they will work in the UK before you buy.

FACILITIES FOR VISITORS WITH DISABILITIES

Many towns on the Costa Blanca have adopted excellent wheelchair-friendly schemes by lowering pavements and removing barriers. Parking for visitors with disabilities is reserved in most areas and stringently enforced by the local police. Some resorts also provide special bathing facilities.

GETTING AROUND

Car hire and driving Reasonably priced car hire is readily available and can often be booked through your tour operator before arrival. If you plan to drive it is worth taking out breakdown insurance with the AA or RAC. Since a disproportionately large number of private cars in Spain often have no insurance, consider fully comprehensive cover rather than plain third party risk. Remember that you will be driving on the right and the standard rule is to give way to traffic from the right, even on roundabouts. Drive carefully and observe all road signs. It is illegal to drive while using a handheld mobile phone and drink driving penalties are severe. For lesser traffic offences, the Spanish Guardia Civil Traffic Police use an on-the-spot fine system and will impound your car if you are unable to pay up immediately.

Public transport Public transport on the Costa Blanca is adequate and inexpensive in coastal areas but sparse inland. Buses and local train services (the *trenet*) link the coastal resorts. The Costa Blanca Express runs between Alicante and Dénia, roughly every hour from 06.00 to 21.00 or 22.00. It stops at many local stations along the way, including Benidorm, Altea, Calpe, Benissa, Gata and Dénia. There is a price reduction for pensioners (you must show your passport). Do not take the word 'express' literally, however; with the single track and the numerous stops, the 80 km (50 mile) journey takes 2 hours and 15 minutes.

Taxis Taxis operate fixed tariffs only within town limits, so agree a price before you start a longer journey.

HEALTH MATTERS

Pharmacists in Spain are authorized to prescribe and supply many restricted drugs over the counter, so it is best to go there first before heading for the hospital or clinic. You will be expected to pay for non-emergency medical treatment even in a public hospital or clinic, although you might be able to reclaim the cost later on your travel insurance. Meanwhile, take obvious precautions to protect yourself from harm.

Health hazards Sunbathe sparingly and never between noon and 16.00, when the sun is at its hottest. Most upset stomachs are caused by a change to the rich Mediterranean diet, so do not overdo it until your body is accustomed to the food on offer.

Water Tap water is generally safe in Spain (most people blame the ice cubes instead of the alcohol), but bottled water (*agua mineral*) is inexpensive and plentiful.

THE LANGUAGE

The Ibicencos respond warmly to visitors who attempt to speak a little of their language. Here are a few words and phrases to get you started:

ENGLISH	**SPANISH** (pronunciation)
General vocabulary	
yes	*sí* (see)
no	*no* (no)
please	*por favor* (por faBOR)
thank you (very much)	*(muchas) gracias* ((MOOchas) GRAtheeyas)
You're welcome	*de nada* (deNAda)
hello	*hola* (Ola)
goodbye	*adiós* (adeeYOS)
good morning/day	*buenos días* (BWEnos DEEyas

ENGLISH	**SPANISH** (pronunciation)

General vocabulary

good afternoon/evening	*buenas tardes* (BWEnas TARdes)
good evening (after dark)	*buenas noches* (BWEnas NOches)
excuse me (to get attention or get past)	*¡disculpe!* (desKOOLpay)
excuse me (to apologize or ask pardon)	*¡perdón!* (perDON)
Sorry	*lo siento* (lo seeYENtoe)
Help!	*¡socorro!* (SOHcohroe)
today	*hoy* (oy)
tomorrow	*mañana* (manYAna)
yesterday	*ayer* (ayYER)

Useful words and phrases

open	*abierto* (abeeYERtoe)
closed	*cerrado* (therRAdoe)
push	*empujar* (empooHAR)
pull	*tirar* (teeRAR)
How much is it?	*¿Cuánto es?* (KWANtoe es)
expensive	*caro/a* (KARo/a)
bank	*el banco* (el BANko)
bureau de change	*la oficina de cambio* (la ofeeTHEEna de KAMbeeyo)
post office	*correos* (koRAYos)
duty (all-night) chemist	*la farmàcia de guardia* (la farMAHtheeya de garDEEya)
bank card	*la tarjeta de banco* (la tarHEHta de BANko)
credit card	*la tarjeta de crédito* (la tarHEHta de CREdeetoe)
travellers' cheques	*los cheques de viaje* (los CHEkes de beeAhay)
table	*la mesa* (la MEHsa)
menu	*el menú/la carta* (el menOO/la KARta)
waiter	*el/la camarero/a* (el/la kahmahRERo/a)

ENGLISH	SPANISH (pronunciation)
Useful words and phrases	
water	*agua* (Agwa)
fizzy/still water	*agua con/sin gas* (Agwa con/sin gas)
I don't understand	*no entiendo* (No enteeYENdoe)
The bill, please	*La cuenta, por favor* (la KWENta, porfaBOR)
Do you speak English?	*¿Habla usted inglés?* (Ablah OOsted eenGLES)
My name is ...	*Me llamo ...* (meh YAmoh ...)
Where are the toilets?	*¿Dónde están los servicios?* (DONdeh esTAN os serBEEtheeos)
Where is there a telephone?	*¿Dónde está un teléfono?* (DONdeh esTAH oon teLEfono)
Can you call me a taxi?	*¿Puede llamar a un taxi?* (PWEday yaMAR ah oon TAKsee)
Can you help me?	*¿Puede ayudarme?* (PWEday ayooDARmeh)

With the exception of the ever-silent 'h' and the silent 'u' between 'g' or 'q' and 'i' or 'e', all letters are pronounced in Spanish. Stress is on the penultimate syllable or on the accented letter (é, for example). English vowel sounds are close enough to suffice.

MEDIA

BBC TV recently reduced its European satellite footprint, blocking transmissions to most of Spain. However, many English language programmes arrive via other channels, including the UK's Channel Five, CNN, Sky News and Eurosport. UK national newspapers are printed in Madrid and available on the Costa on the same day. The award-winning English language *Costa Blanca News* is published weekly and covers all local and national news, entertainment and notices of local fiestas and attractions. Radio Onda Cero International (94.6 FM) and Spectrum Radio (88.2 FM) are English language radio stations with links to BBC World News throughout the day.

⬤ *Eating alfresco is one of the pleasures of dining out*

OPENING HOURS

Smaller shops and businesses in Spain follow the custom of the siesta, closing between 13.30 and 16.00 and staying open until 19.30 or 20.00 Monday to Friday and closing Saturday afternoon and all day Sunday. Larger department stores and hypermarkets are usually open all day and some remain open on Sundays during the high season. Banks are open to the public from 09.00 to 16.00 Monday to Friday, with Saturday morning opening confined to the winter months, although most have 24-hour cashpoints that will accept UK cash cards. Pharmacies operate the siesta system, but will always display the address of an emergency 24-hour pharmacist in the area. Check out the opening times of places of interest with the local information office, especially for national and local public holidays, of which Spain has more than anywhere else in Europe. The Spanish eat late, with most restaurants opening at 20.00 and serving dinner until midnight.

PERSONAL COMFORT & SECURITY

Every company, shop, restaurant and bar in Spain is required to hold a Complaints Register (*Libro de Reclamaciones*), which is regularly inspected by the local authorities. Complaints to the police are called '*denuncias*' and are accompanied by much form filling, especially in the case of theft. Be sensible and you will save yourself the trouble.

Your hotel will usually undertake your dry cleaning and laundry, although most holiday resorts have cleaners and laundrettes. Take enough clothes to save yourself the bother.

All bars provide toilets (*los servicios*) that members of the public may use, although it is considered polite to fit it in with a stop for coffee or a glass of wine. Other places providing the service are railway stations and bus terminals, but do not waste your time looking for a council public toilet – there are none.

If you lose property in the street, try the local police station, although bar, restaurant and shop assistants will usually hold onto the item in case you return, so try to remember where you lost it. Do not 'lose' your bag or wallet accidentally by leaving it unattended.

In Spain, theft comes under two categories, '*robo*' and '*hurto*'. The former involves some form of bodily contact such as bag-snatching. The latter refers to stealing an unguarded item. Insurance companies generally regard the latter as your own fault and refuse to pay compensation. Whatever the occurrence, always make a complaint (*denuncia*) to the police to support your claim.

Airports and resorts all over the world attract criminals, so be on your guard. If you are travelling with a tour group, take your luggage to the coach and stay with it until it is loaded. If you have chosen car hire, ask the desk representative to take you to your vehicle. They may refuse if they are busy, in which case refuse all other help from anyone loitering in the car park.

Leave all your valuables and spare cash in the hotel safe when registering. Your travel insurance may be void if you do not. The Costa Blanca crime rate is no worse and a lot better than many holiday destinations, but be alert and take sensible precautions as you would at home.

POST OFFICES

These are called 'correos' and exist in every town and village, but stamps can also be purchased in state tobacco shops, kiosks and shops that sell postcards. The usual services are available at post office counters, which are open from 10.00 to 14.00 Monday to Friday.

RELIGION

Spain is a Catholic country, although because of immigration and foreign residency churches of most denominations abound. The British Anglican community is particularly strong on the Costa Blanca. The English language newspaper *Costa Blanca News* carries a weekly list of church services for all denominations.

TELEPHONES

There are numerous telephone booths dotted around where you can make calls with credit cards or using coins. Please be warned that if you are using coins, you will need lots of them. Calls can also be made from your hotel room, but this is an expensive option. Telefonica is the main telephone company and it generally has several kiosks in tourist areas where you can make metered calls and then pay an attendant afterwards. This is generally the most economical way of making telephone calls to the UK.

TIME DIFFERENCES

Mainland Spain is always an hour ahead of the UK and changes its clocks forward and backwards according to GMT and BST with an hour added.

PHONING ABROAD

To call the UK dial **oo** and wait for the dialling tone to change. Then dial **44** (the country code) and the area code (minus the first o) followed by the number. The country code for Ireland is **353**.

TIPPING

The Spanish service industry is reliant on tips and it is customary to leave a few cents on the bar when you pay for a beer or coffee. In restaurants, the norm is around 15 per cent of the bill. Taxi drivers expect around 10 per cent.

WEIGHTS & MEASUREMENTS

Spain uses the metric system, so you will be dealing with kilos, litres and centimetres. Some clothes and shoes may carry the equivalent UK sizes, but these can differ enormously so always ask to try something on if you can and use a measures converter (look in your pocket diary) for reference.

When out enjoying yourself, remember that a Spanish single measure of alcohol is equivalent to at least a British treble measure and save yourself a hangover.

Imperial to metric

1 inch = 2.54 centimetres
1 foot = 30 centimetres
1 yard = 0.9 metres
1 mile = 1.6 kilometres
1 ounce = 28 grams
1 pound = 454 grams

Metric to imperial

1 centimetre = 0.4 inches
1 metre = 3 feet, 3 inches
1 kilometre = 0.6 miles
1 gram = 0.04 ounces
1 kilogram = 2.2 pounds
1 litre = 1.8 pints

ACKNOWLEDGEMENTS

We would like to thank all the photographers, picture libraries and organisations for the loan of the photographs reproduced in this book, to whom copyright in the photograph belongs:
Donna Dailey (pages 12, 17, 18, 45, 93, 103);
Jupiter Images Corporation (pages 109, 125);
Pictures Colour Library Ltd (pages 11, 33, 34, 39, 43, 44, 47, 48, 52, 69, 75, 77, 84, 90, 97, 100, 121);
Spanish Tourist Office (page 67);
Terra Mítica (page 27);
Thomas Cook Tour Operations Ltd (pages 1, 5, 26, 29, 37, 61, 65, 71, 95, 105, 107, 108).

We would also like to thank the following for their contribution to this series:
John Woodcock (map and symbols artwork);
Becky Alexander, Patricia Baker, Sophie Bevan, Judith Chamberlain-Webber, Nicky Gyopari, Stephanie Horner, Krystyna Mayer, Robin Pridy (editorial support);
Christine Engert, Suzie Johanson, Richard Lloyd, Richard Peters, Alistair Plumb, Jane Prior, Barbara Theisen, Ginny Zeal, Barbara Zuñiga (Design support).

Send your thoughts to
books@thomascook.com

* Found a beach bar, peaceful stretch of sand or must-see sight that we don't feature?

* Like to tip us off about any information that needs a little updating?

* Want to tell us what you love about this handy, little guidebook and more importantly how we can make it even handier?

Then here's your chance to tell all! Send us ideas, discoveries and recommendations today and then look out for your valuable input in the next edition of this title. And, as an extra 'thank you' from Thomas Cook Publishing, you'll be automatically entered into our exciting monthly prize draw.

Email to the above address or write to:
HotSpots Project Editor, Thomas Cook Publishing, PO Box 227, Unit 15/16, Coningsby Road, Peterborough PE3 8SB, UK.